LET THE
POEMS BEGIN!

A POET'S GUIDE TO WRITING POETRY

Written by Gene Fehler
Illustrated by Tani Brooks Johnson

Good Apple
A Division of Frank Schaffer Publications, Inc.

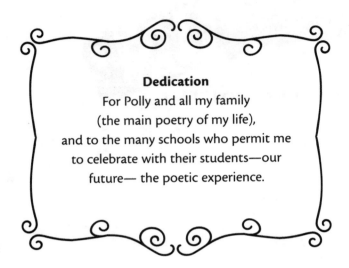

Dedication
For Polly and all my family
(the main poetry of my life),
and to the many schools who permit me
to celebrate with their students—our
future— the poetic experience.

Editors: Joanne Corker, Kristin Eclov, Christine Hood, Michael Batty

Book Design: Rose Sheifer Graphic Productions

Graphic Artist: Anthony Strasburger

Good Apple
A Division of Frank Schaffer Publications, Inc.
23740 Hawthorne Boulevard
Torrance, CA 90505

Table of Contents

Table of Contents (continued)

Introduction

Let the Poems Begin! is an intriguing anthology of over 100 captivating poems. It is not an academic tome of grammar and poetic theory. Rather, its pages offer teachers and students a fresh approach to reading and writing poems—a way to look at poetry from a personal perspective.

Using a friendly, conversational approach, the author shares personal insights and practical suggestions about writing poetry. The accessible nature of the poems demonstrates that writing a poem is an attainable goal, that poetry isn't something to be feared, and that searching out poetry books at libraries and bookstores might actually be fun. Each chapter also includes motivating writing opportunities to encourage young poets in their poetic endeavors.

Let the Poems Begin! is written for everyone who has ever or never tried to write a poem. It is designed for all those individuals who think poetry is boring or outdated or too difficult to understand. This book is for *all* prospective poets!

 ## What Is the Purpose of This Book?

The background information, teaching tips, poems, and writing opportunities in this book are intended to show some of the specific thoughts or experiences that generate poems, and give examples of poems that:

- share experiences.

- tell stories.

- use language in a unique way.

- create various moods.

- give fresh insights into human nature.

- suggest lessons about life.

- help show ideas, objects, places, and people in entirely new ways.

- satirize something or someone.

- imitate the style of other poems.

- entertain.

- help you experience a wide range of emotions as you read poetry.

- show that you can write a poem—a good poem—if you truly want to!

Teacher Pages

TEACHING POINTS

Using an honest and open style, teacher pages present easy-to-understand information and teaching points about the reading and writing of poetry. You can share these pages directly with students, enjoying the clear facts and thought-provoking insights together.

POETIC PRINCIPLES

At the bottom of each teacher page, you will find an important principle or generalization from that chapter. These concepts reflect my feelings about poetry. Share these principles with students and invite them to discuss each concept. Your students can also record these generalizations in their poetry journals and create posters or memos to highlight favorite ideas.

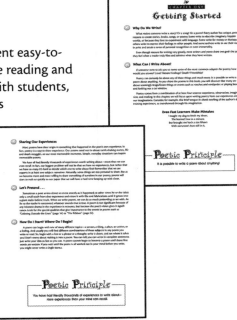

Student Pages (to be reproduced)

A WORD FROM THE POET

Most student pages include at least one of these short and friendly conversations. In these paragraphs, I share how I developed ideas for specific poems and how I wrote my thoughts as rhyme or free verse. I also mention questions I may have asked myself and techniques I may have used as I revised my poems and perfected my writing.

POEMS

These poems include a mixture of light, serious, fixed form, and free verse. They deal with a wide range of topics, including many sports poems. There are also a few rough drafts to illustrate specific aspects of the revision process.

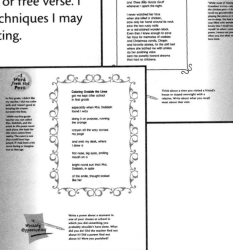

Challenging and enjoyable writing opportunities follow most poems. You can use these ideas as springboards to encourage students to experiment with writing their own forms of rhymed, fixed, and free verse. As students focus on these writing opportunities throughout the year, they will begin to develop a significant body of rough poetry drafts—and become budding poets.

Appendix

The concluding pages of the appendix include a list of definitions for many common poetic terms. There is also an alphabetical listing of all poems found in the book to help you locate specific titles, and a page of publication credits for previously published poems.

How Do I Use This Book?

As a teacher or student who is interested in poetry, you can read each chapter from beginning to end and gain a comprehensive introduction to the poetic experience. Or, you can select poems and activities from virtually any part of the book and prepare classroom lessons on different aspects of poetry. You can use this book with individual students for independent study and with small or whole-class groups.

Each teacher and student page can be used directly with students. You can make copies of student pages and appropriate teacher pages and use them with the whole class or with individual students. You can also make overhead transparencies of selected pages to highlight specific teaching points.

Encourage students to begin their own loose-leaf poetry journals or notebooks. They can record lists with ideas for writing poems, first lines or phrases that they might want to use, first and ongoing drafts of their poems, reactions to poetic principles, and student pages from this book with the author's poems and writing opportunities. Also, encourage students to experiment with and create original ways to "print" and "publish" their completed poems.

Let the Poems Begin!

Remember, this book is designed to help students realize that poetry can be fun and is easier to write than they may have imagined. So take a breath, for you are about to begin a marvelous poetic journey! Let the poems begin!

CHAPTER ONE

Getting Started

Why Do We Write?

What makes someone write a story? a song? a poem? Every author has unique, personal reasons to create stories, books, songs, or poetry. Some write to describe imaginary, happier worlds, or because they love to experiment with language. Some write for money or therapy; others write to express their feelings to other people. And some authors write to see their names in print and attain a sense of personal recognition or even immortality.

Even though reasons for writing vary greatly, most writers and poets share one goal—the joy they feel when a reader truly likes and admires what they have written.

What Can I Write About?

If someone were to ask you to name some of the most common subjects for poetry, how would you answer? Love? Nature? Feelings? Death? Friendship?

Poetry can certainly be about any of these things and much more. It is possible to write a poem about anything. As you share the poems in this book, you will discover that many are about seemingly insignificant things or events, such as roaches and centipedes or playing baseball and looking out a car window.

Poetry comes from a combination of at least four sources: experience, observation, imagination, and reading. In this chapter, we will focus on writing poetry from our experiences and imaginations. Consider, for example, this brief tongue-in-cheek retelling of my dog-training experiences, as transformed through my imagination.

Even Fast Learners Make Mistakes

I taught my dog to fetch my shoes;
She learned how in a minute,
But brought me back a size fifteen
With someone's foot still in it.

—Gene Fehler

Poetic Principle

It is possible to write a poem about anything!

⚇ Sharing Experiences

Most poems have their origin in something that happened in the poet's own experience. In fact, poetry is a way to share experiences. Poems need not be about earth-shaking events, life and death struggles, or most memorable moments. Simple, everyday situations can inspire memorable poems.

We have all had literally thousands of experiences worth writing about—more than we can even recall. In fact, our biggest problem will not be that we have no experiences, but rather that we have so many it's hard to decide which one to write about first! Remember, we are experts in at least one subject—ourselves. Naturally, some things are too personal to share. But as we become more and more willing to share something of ourselves in our poetry, poems will start to rush out so quickly that we will have a hard time keeping up with them.

⚇ Let's Pretend . . .

Sometimes a poet writes about an event exactly as it happened; other times, he or she takes only a small truth from that experience and mixes it with fibs and fabrications until it grows into a giant make-believe truth. When we write poems, we can do as much pretending as we wish. As far as the reader is concerned, whatever sounds true *is* true. A poem is not significant because of any inherent drama in the experience it recounts, but because the poet's vision gives it significance. Look for the special qualities that give importance to the events in poems such as "Coloring Outside the Lines" (page 10) or "The Ribbon" (page 20).

⚇ How Do I Start? Where Do I Begin?

A poem can begin with one of many different topics—a person, a thing, a place, an action, or a feeling. And usually you will find different combinations of these subjects in any poem you write or read. So, begin with a line, a phrase, or a thought; write it down, and see where it takes you! Don't worry about making it into a poem. You can tell; you can write in complete sentences; just write your ideas as fast as you can. A poem cannot begin to become a poem until those first words are written. If you wait until the poem is all worked out in your mind before you write, you may never write a single stanza.

Poetic Principle

You have had literally thousands of experiences to write about— more experiences than your mind can recall.

Simple Guidelines and First Steps

Use these practical tips to help you write great poems:

- When you write about a person, describe the individual and show where he or she is or what he or she is doing.

- When you write about a place, identify a specific setting. Picture it clearly in your mind and choose words that let the reader see the same things you see.

- When you write about a thing, consider what the object looks like or reminds you of. Find a new or unusual way to describe it; try to compare it to something else (simile or metaphor). Talk about where the object is, what it is doing, or what someone is doing with it.

- When you write about an action, describe it as vividly as possible. Use strong, active verbs. For example, instead of writing *It rained hard*, let the rain take the action—*Rain hammered the windows; water raced in the gutters; rain blew in sheets across the highway, drowning his windshield wipers.*

- When you write about a time, identify a specific moment. It can be from your past; a moment that might have happened, but didn't; or one that you wish had happened.

 ## What Next?

Once you have written your first draft, ask yourself this question: *Am I happy with this as a complete poem, or do I want to make it longer?* If you decide to build your idea into a longer poem, you might consider one or more of these suggestions:

- Use a fresh or startling image to describe something.

- Make a surprising statement.

- Tell a story.

- Compare one thing to something else.

- Build the mood.

- Show how you feel (try to make the reader feel a certain way).

- Add another person to the poem.

When you write a poem, you can do as much
pretending as you wish.

As you start to make changes, your words will begin to become a poem. Remember that when you write, you don't have to put everything in. Sometimes the words say too much (and sometimes not enough). Leave out everything that does not relate directly to the moment or mood you want to capture in your poem.

 ## Should My Poems Rhyme?

Many readers feel that poetry has to rhyme. However, most poems written and published today are free verse poems; they contain no definite rhyme or rhythmic pattern. "Dinner for Three" (page 25) is a rhymed poem and "Night of the Centipedes" (page 11) is not. Is rhyme necessary? Of course not. Is rhyme desirable? Yes and no.

How do writers decide whether or not to rhyme their poems? Poets often write first drafts in free verse. Then they ask themselves if they feel happy with their ideas or if they might work better as rhymed poems. Ideas that are free verse in their first draft often become rhymed poems in later versions.

For example, I once wrote about an experience I had on a tire swing. I wrote first in free verse, intending merely to record the essence of the experience as quickly as possible.

Tire Swing (first draft)

Aaron swung me high and hard.
My screams startled flying birds
then swallowed me on my downward sweep.
I lurched sideways,
jerking the rope toward me.
My matchstick legs scratched
the oak's matchbox bark.
Blood spread like flames
across dry August air,
past Aaron's arms flung wide,
trying to bring me back.

—Gene Fehler

I felt dissatisfied with this poem, so I decided to experiment with rhyme. I developed a new first line that just happened to have the rhythm of a sonnet (see page 67). I decided to use sonnet form. As I worked through the process of revising the form of my poem, my ideas also changed shape.

Poetic Principle

If you wait until a poem is all worked out in your mind
before you write, you may never write a single stanza.

Tire Swing (final draft)

My brother Aaron swung me high and hard
Toward tops of trees, until I almost flew
Into the blue of sky above our yard.
I peaked, then roller-coasted down and through
My squeals that sprinkled on the distant ground.
I tilted, lurched, then fought to grab the rope
And stop my fall. The tire spun around
With wild abandon. I could only hope
That God or Aaron (either one would do)
Could soften up the oak tree's matchbox bark
Which planned a terrifying rendezvous
Somewhere within the tire's final arc.
I closed my eyes and never found out why
The oak tree stepped aside to let me by.

—Gene Fehler

Is the sonnet version of the tire swing experience better than the free verse version? There's no absolutely right or wrong answer. Sometimes poets begin with the intent to write a fixed form poem (e.g., quatrain, limerick, sonnet, sestina), but find themselves too restricted by its rules. At other times, poets start with free verse form, but begin to play with rhymes that randomly appear. Look for examples of both free verse and fixed forms throughout this book.

And Now for Some Poems

The remainder of this chapter presents a selection of poems that have come from my "undramatic" everyday experiences. They share memories of visits with Grandma, encounters with centipedes, and triumphs at high school track meets. Some of these poems are almost entirely true, others less so. However, they all use inspiration from my experiences and imagination to create poems that seem real and authentic to the reader.

Most poems include one or more writing opportunities for you to share your own experiences. Remember that how you decide to present your story or memory will determine whether it seems real or true to your readers, and whether they attach any significance to it.

Poetic Principle

Poetry is a way to share experiences.

Seeing Grandma

Grandma chased chickens,
hatchet in hand,
dragged one squawking
to the chopping block—
Grandma, who never raised
her voice in anger,
who made me soft, warm
peanut butter cookies,
who played Christmas carols
and Chopin on her piano,
who read me to sleep with
The Little Engine That Could
and *Three Billy Goats Gruff*
whenever I spent the night.

I never watched her face
when she killed a chicken,
saw only her hand around its neck,
saw the two rusty nails
on a red-stained wooden block.
Even then I knew enough to save
her face for memories of cookies
and Christmas carols, Chopin
and favorite stories, for the soft bed
where she bathed me with smiles
as her soothing voice
sent me sweetly toward dreams
that had no chickens.

—Gene Fehler

A Word from the Poet

" When I was little, my parents would occasionally let me stay overnight at my grandparents' house. Some of the things I recall most are my grandmother baking cookies, playing cards and checkers with me, and killing a chicken for Sunday dinner.

"While most of 'Seeing Grandma' is true—especially the chicken part—I don't recall my grandmother ever playing the piano or reading me to sleep. She had a book-case filled with wonderful books that I recall reading to myself. So when I wrote the poem, I wrote not precisely what *was*, but what *might have been*. "

Writing Opportunity

Think about a time you visited a friend's house or stayed overnight with a relative. Write about what you recall most about that visit.

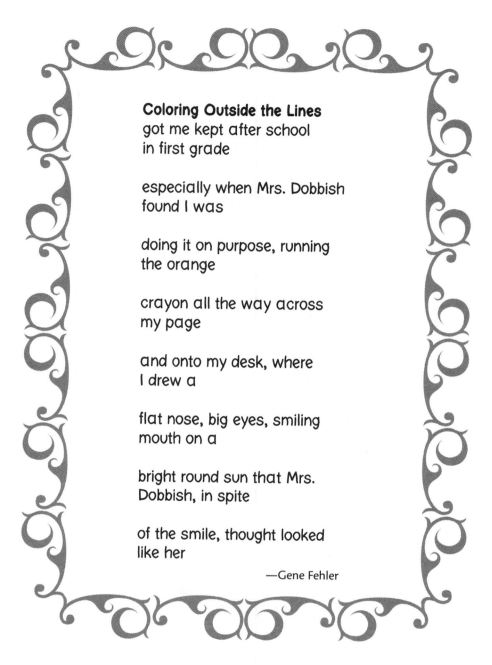

"While my first-grade teacher was not called Mrs. Dobbish, and the event in this poem never took place, the basis for this story comes from reality. The event is one that could have happened if I had been a bit more daring or imaginative at that age."**99**

Coloring Outside the Lines
got me kept after school
in first grade

especially when Mrs. Dobbish
found I was

doing it on purpose, running
the orange

crayon all the way across
my page

and onto my desk, where
I drew a

flat nose, big eyes, smiling
mouth on a

bright round sun that Mrs.
Dobbish, in spite

of the smile, thought looked
like her

—Gene Fehler

Writing Opportunity

Write a poem about a moment in one of your classes at school in which you did something you probably shouldn't have done. What did you do? Did the teacher find out about it? Did a parent find out about it? Were you punished?

Night of the Centipedes
Track stars on my bedroom walls.
I called them enemy, war-mongers,
moderators of nightmares.
I screamed for reinforcements,
dug a blanketed foxhole,
did not see Mom take aim
with bazooka newspaper.
I heard explosions,
peeked from covers to see
new roses on daisy'd wallpaper.
Mom kissed my forehead.
I wished her to stay,
but I dared not tell her.
Eyelids frozen, I fought sleep.
Clattering beyond my pillow
were dreams of bloody legs.

—Gene Fehler

" When I was ten years old, my parents bought a house. It was old, and I suppose it was even bordering on run-down, but to me it was wonderful. It had two special qualities: it belonged to us, not to a landlord; and it had an indoor bathroom, something that our previous rented house did not have.

"My elation at moving to our own home turned quickly to horror on the first night there. While lying in bed, I saw a strange creature crawl through the shadows on my wall. Then I saw another and another! I reached for the light next to my bed and flicked it on. Centipedes! I was so afraid of them that I couldn't even kill them. They ran so fast I was afraid one would crawl up my arm before I could smash it with a shoe or newspaper.

"My poem 'Night of the Centipedes' is an actual account of the way I felt that night and how I was saved from the centipedes. There's no pretending here. **"**

Writing Opportunity

The dark of night often magnifies our small fears into giant ones and our large fears into monstrous ones. Try to remember a specific night when one of your own fears (real or imagined) became magnified into terror (e.g., alone in your house, walking down a dark street, camping in the woods). Now share your story.

❝ My grandfather was the township road commissioner. I often rode in the front seat with him when he drove to get a load of gravel.

"The events in this poem happened pretty much as I describe them. Of course, there's much about my grandfather that I left out. Also, it's not important that I mention how disgusting the act of chewing tobacco and spitting it out might seem to me or to others. All that's important for the poem is my recollection of the joy of riding in that big truck and the remarkable ability my grandfather had to hit that coffee can! ❞

The Marksman
Of all the things
I loved about my grandad

the best was not the fact
that he let me sit next to him
on the front seat of the township truck

when he drove to the quarry
for a load of gravel

but the way his spray
of sweet-smelling chewing tobacco
sailed over my lap

while we bounced over country roads
at forty miles an hour

and pinged dead center
in the coffee can

every time.

—Gene Fehler

Writing Opportunity

Think about a relative who had an unusual characteristic or habit. Write a poem about that person.

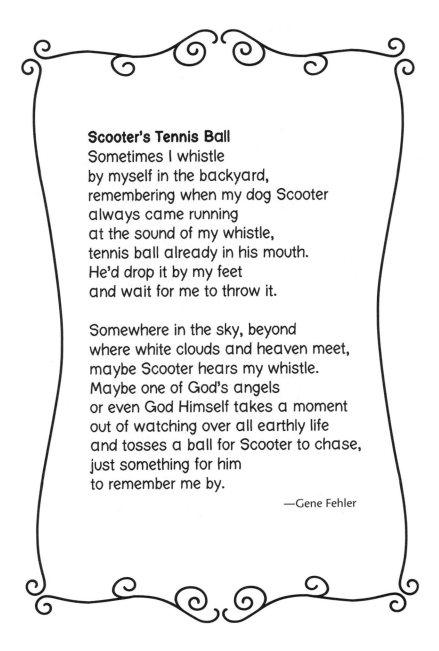

Scooter's Tennis Ball

Sometimes I whistle
by myself in the backyard,
remembering when my dog Scooter
always came running
at the sound of my whistle,
tennis ball already in his mouth.
He'd drop it by my feet
and wait for me to throw it.

Somewhere in the sky, beyond
where white clouds and heaven meet,
maybe Scooter hears my whistle.
Maybe one of God's angels
or even God Himself takes a moment
out of watching over all earthly life
and tosses a ball for Scooter to chase,
just something for him
to remember me by.

—Gene Fehler

A Word from the Poet

❝ I never had a dog while I was growing up, but my friend Johnny did. His dog was named Jack, and he could catch a ball in mid-air with the best of them.

"I have a dog now and know the pain of just contemplating her possible death. If my dog should die before I do, I'd like to believe that she will be in a place where she can remember me as fondly as I will her. ❞

Writing Opportunity

Write about a time when you experienced the death of a pet, someone else's pet, a friend, a relative, or any animal (perhaps you saw it on the highway and didn't know who it belonged to). Perhaps you were in an accident or were ill and almost died. Death is painful to think about, but sometimes writing about our thoughts can make us feel just a little better.

66 My dad broke his back and was hospitalized for a while. At the end of this poem I imply something worse than what really happened. **99**

The Silence

I was six, my sister seven,
racing through giggles in our living room
when the knock came. The words
(from Dad's friend, I knew the voice)
knifed their way past Mom
through the shadowy doorway
toward our laughter which never let up
as the thrust of the words missed us:
". . . fall . . . grain elevator . . .
hospital . . . broken neck. . . ."

Mom rushed out with him,
shouting for old Mrs. Rutherford
from across the street to stay with us.
All afternoon her pinched eyes
hovered over us, but my sister and I
kept playing and giggling
until our front door opened so softly
it took my breath away. I stared
as the silence that filled Mom's face
crept toward us
and swallowed our laughter.

—Gene Fehler

Writing Opportunity

Imagine a moment of great silence. Describe the circumstances in which the silence presents itself. Suggest something about your feelings in that silence.

REPRODUCIBLE

Ribbon of Letters

Three miles from home
on a strange road
at the edge of woods
seldom visited,
the house stood silent,
dusty windows webbed
across the crack of glass.

Curt and I, coming home
from fishing,
stopped to explore.
The inside—empty,
except for a tilted table,
two wooden chairs,
a broken chest of drawers.

The drawers contained
only spiders and this:
a packet of yellowed letters,
tied by red ribbon.
I reached for them,
was chilled by what felt
like a whisper.
We left the letters
untouched, undisturbed
bones in a coffin.

—Gene Fehler

Writing Opportunity

Write a poem about one of your own experiences. Select an event you don't think many of your friends have experienced. Try to show your readers exactly what you saw and did, what you thought, and how you felt. Remember: It doesn't have to be true; you can make things up.

A Word from the Poet

66 Almost everyone has gone to school with a bully. My school had one whom I will call 'Bennie.' Each year from grades 5 through 8, our class took a full-day class trip. That day was the highlight of the year. I remember my eighth-grade class trip for three reasons—burning my tongue while drinking boiling hot cocoa at our breakfast stop, sitting with a girl named Judy, and the moment our bus left school in the morning. Even today I'm not sure whether the event (Bennie missing the bus) really happened or whether I merely dreamed it. **99**

The Day Bennie Missed the Bus

Giggling in the five A.M. darkness,
we rushed for the school bus,
eighth-grade adventurers
ready to travel across civilized plains
to where Chicago's wilds waited.
We piled on, Dale and Connie,
Judy and me packed in back,
shoulders touching already.
Miss Hasting counted heads:
twenty-eight . . . twenty-nine . . .
thirty . . . only one student missing.

Bennie was not there.
Slow Bennie, the school bully.
Bennie the loner.

Miss Hasting took a last look outside.
"It's time," she said
to the accompaniment of thirty cheers.
The bus pulled out,
headlights cutting a path toward Chicago,
leaving behind us the empty schoolyard swings
and Bennie running into sight now,
arms waving in frenzied pantomime.
I watched his arms drop to his sides
as we turned the next corner,
and I never told anyone he was there.

—Gene Fehler

❝ Some readers think the narrator in this poem is a rotten person—that he has no decency, compassion, or concern for his fellow man. Others feel that the narrator was smart, since Bennie would have ruined the whole trip for everybody. How I as the poet feel about the narrator's silence is totally irrelevant. How the reader feels is what is important, and there is no right or wrong way for the reader to feel. ❞

Writing Opportunity

A rough paraphrase of "The Day Bennie Missed the Bus" might read like this:

Our eighth-grade class met at five A.M. in the school playground to wait for a bus that would take us to Chicago for our class trip. We got on the bus. I sat in the back with Judy as Miss Hasting counted to see if everybody was there. Bennie, the school bully, was the only one absent. Miss Hasting looked outside and then told the bus driver to leave. I looked out the back window and saw Bennie. I had to decide whether or not to tell anybody. I decided not to tell.

Write a brief prose summary of a personal experience, similar in length to the "Bennie" poem. This will be your rough draft for a poem. Then take a line or two of that summary and revise it so that instead of *telling* about the experience, you are *showing*. For example, the poet shows how excited the class is about the trip by using words such as *giggling, rushed for the school bus, adventurers,* and *piled on.*

Now, try your hand at making your prose into a poem.

Reunion with the Town Bully

Eating the five P.M. Thursday Night Special,
we sat, Dad and I, in the village's only cafe
that second day of my last trip back home.
I had practically lived there
when Roy and Jessie owned it,
twenty-plus years before,
those half-forgotten high school summer nights
of vanilla phosphates and jukebox Elvis.

Now, halfway through dessert,
the booming voice: "Hey! How's it going?"
A voice from twenty years in the past,
yet I knew it from the many fights we had,
from countless times teachers sought to subdue it.

"Hi, Bennie," I muttered, rising to accept
his outstretched hand with my own.
He towered over me still, a mountain,
still grinning his childlike grin.

He asked about me. Was I married? Any kids?
Strangers listening would have thought us
long lost best friends finally reunited.
"Bennie's the hardest worker in town,"
Dad said later. "Not too smart,
but he'd give you the shirt off his back."
I recalled my own back, and sides, and face,
bruised and bloodied all too often,
and I only nodded when Dad added,
"They don't come any better than old Bennie."

—Gene Fehler

Writing Opportunity

Select one of your previously written poems and write a sequel to it. Follow-up on some aspect of the poem—perhaps a character or the setting—that the reader might be interested in reading about again.

Hero Worship

the day Donnie's cute cousin
came to visit
I was uncanny
while she watched
from the grass of courtside
our summer basketball
I spun left through a crowd
laying it home for two.
moments later I popped net
from thirty,
pretended she wasn't there
stole a pass
hooked it in from the right
wondering
how she could keep the cheers
bottled inside
I soared for a rebound
hit a baseline jumper
not missing once
until I saw her stroll away
hand in hand
with Ralph Boone, the sissy
from down the street
who was ugly besides

—Gene Fehler

❝ One high school summer, I was playing a game of school yard basketball. I showed off, trying to impress my friend Donnie's cousin, Carol. I was sure that when she saw me on the basketball court, she'd fall in love with me.

"On this particular day, I actually played one of the best basketball games ever, not missing a single shot and doing everything wonderfully. But Carol walked off with somebody else whose name I changed. Was Ralph a sissy or ugly? Probably not, but in my state of mind I wasn't going to find anything good to say about him!

"Unfortunately, this poem is as true as any I've ever written. I could have added how my game deteriorated after Carol left, but thought it would be better to end with them walking off. ❞

Writing Opportunity

Recall a time when you tried to show off to impress someone. What did you do? Whom were you trying to impress? What was the outcome of your attempt to show off? Write a poem about this experience.

The Ribbon

In our county meet back in eighth grade,
my longest jump was thirteen feet,
nine and a half inches,
good enough for a fifth place tie.

I watched them hand out ribbons: blue,
red, white, yellow. Eager hands peeled
them from the cool air of spring's dusk.
I saw the ribbon for fifth place.

It was bright green. I could almost feel
its gloss between my thumb and fingertips.
But there were no extra green ribbons;
they would have to flip a coin.

The other boy, tall and freckled, stammered
a quiet "t-t-tails." The air caught both the spinning
coin and my breath, held one and threw the other
toward the meet director's powerful hand.

I still have the ribbon.
I wonder if the other boy remembers that coin
spinning, or dreams of that narrow piece
of silk, new and bright green.

—Gene Fehler

Writing Opportunity

Write a poem about a time when you won—or lost—at something. It may have been a sporting event or a game with a family member. You may have been part of a team or alone. Did you do anything special that contributed to the win or loss? How did you feel after winning or losing? What special things do you recall about what your opponent(s) did or how your opponent(s) felt?

Dance of the Darkroom

At the high school sock hop, Johnny and I
sneaked away from our dates to the darkroom
next to the physics lab where Mr. Brooks
        kept his radio.
Music from the gym seeped through old
        floorboards,
too softly, though, to drown out the NCAA
        basketball
championship play-by-play of LaSalle–Iowa,
sweeter to my ears than any love song.
If our dates missed us on the dance floor
that hour or so, they never said.
But to Mom's question, "How was the dance?"
I grinned and said in truth, "The best ever."
There's no way she could hide her sudden smile.
I knew how happy she was at the progress
being made by her son, the wallflower.

—Gene Fehler

❝ At a high school dance, my best friend and I left our girlfriends alone while we listened to a basketball game on the radio. If you read a history of college basketball, you can even find out what year that LaSalle–Iowa game took place.

"What is not true, however, is my mom's question. I don't recall the events of the last five lines taking place. But they could have! If my mom had asked that question, I would have answered the same way. And my mom would have smiled, because I was socially inept, a 'wall-flower'; and my mother fervently hoped that I might someday blossom. ❞

Writing Opportunity

Write a poem about something you did that made a parent, teacher, or friend proud of you. It doesn't matter whether you think you deserved the praise or not; all that matters is that the other person said you did.

Shy Admirer

I've seen the damage words can do—
Words in song, in speech, in book,
    To name a few.

Yet far, far worse is all the joy I never knew
Because of words I couldn't bring myself
    To say to you.

—Gene Fehler

Hi

Writing Opportunity

Think about something you have been wanting to do. It might be something at school or at home or with your friends. What might happen if you did this special deed? Put your thoughts or dreams into a poem. Try to include at least one line of dialogue.

How He Sometimes Graded History Essays

That last year in academia,
before they refused him tenure,
he'd give a toss from the top of the stairs
and an accident of fate
gave some students' words weight
enough to reach the bottom (an A).
Some stayed toward the middle (B, C),
some higher (D, F).

The highest was lowest
in his joyously perverse grading mystery
when gravity was the key
to passing history.

—Gene Fehler

A Word from the Poet

❝ Sometimes poems can be written about embarrassing moments. My first year out of college I was teaching English at a high school in Illinois. Of course, I always had a stack of student essays that needed grading. One evening my roommate, Bill, a history teacher at the school, wanted me to go bowling with him. I told him I couldn't—I had student essays to grade and hand back the next day.

"Bill took my stack of essays, stood at the top of the stairs, and gave them a toss. Then he walked down the steps, writing grades *A* to *F* in his red marking pen on the papers . 'Now they're graded,' he said. 'Let's go bowling.'

"I did go bowling. But I also regraded the papers before I handed them back. I had some explaining to do when students asked questions like, 'Why did you cross out the A and give me a C–?'

"In this poem, I changed the reality of the experience, but kept the act of 'grading by the tossing method' a key part of the story. ❞

Writing Opportunity

Write a poem in which you pay tribute, either seriously or humorously, to someone you admire.

Jogging in Winter
Beaded sweat like pinheads
froze
this morning where my red beard
reached
to touch winter. I jogged through a
hush
of dawn trailing me; my breath
puffed
like periods between fragmented
sentences
hoping to become a four-mile essay.

—Gene Fehler

❝ In my entire life, I grew a beard only once—a nice, thick, red beard—and shaved it off after six months. But I happened to have that beard during one season of jogging when I was teaching English at Kishwaukee College in Illinois. I was living in a country house and could see the college three miles away across snowy winter cornfields. The route of my morning jog was a four-mile square on a country dirt road.

"My purpose in this poem was to merely describe that freezing winter morning jog as clearly as I could. ❞

Writing
Opportunity

Describe a time when you experienced colder-than-normal temperatures. Where were you? When did it happen? How cold was it? How were you or your family affected?

Dinner for Three

My food was fine (without reproach)
As I sat down alone to eat
When suddenly an ugly roach
Appeared and pranced across my meat.

And as I scowled with dark disgust
And raised in haste my sharpened knife,
Another nibbled my bread crust:
It might have been the first one's wife.

I made my move to snuff them out
Forever with a deadly crunch,
Then stopped. A voice (God's voice, no doubt),
Said, "Every creature needs a lunch."

Well. Those poor creatures looked forlorn
While sniffing at my well-filled plate.
It wasn't their fault they were born
As roaches, so we sat and ate.

—Gene Fehler

66 Some years ago, we decided to leave Illinois and go live in Alabama. Our move brought many exciting discoveries, including our first close look at the local roaches. Although these gigantic, brownish-red creatures reminded us of the June bugs we had disliked in Illinois, they seemed nastier somehow.

"To this day, my wife Polly ranks these roaches among the most despicable of creatures, so I wrote this roach poem for her! But I'm happy to say that the situation I describe in 'Dinner for Three' did not happen—I made it up. **99**

Writing Opportunity

Most of us spend several hours a week at the dinner, lunch, or breakfast table. Take some time to think about special moments that have taken place there—pleasant conversations, arguments, smells and tastes of delicious or terrible food, disappointments, and laughter.

Allow the reader to be your dinner guest as you capture the essence of the experience in a poem. You might even write about the after-dinner experience of clearing the table and washing and drying the dishes.

66 The following poem is based on an actual experience, but I was not one of its youthful 'heroes.' I was the husband of the mother, and the heroes were my two sons. Tim and Andy performed this feat when they were in middle school while we were living in Montgomery, Alabama. 99

An Evening of Roach Killing

We sprayed the house;
Then, protected by Dad's steel-toed boots,
Armed with grenades of bug spray,
We attacked the crawling sewer cover
In the vacant lot next door.
We counted two hundred forty victims.

Pacifists. Both of us.
We never shot squirrels or birds,
Never squished summer fireflies
To make our fingernails glow.
We squirmed at the sight
Of collections of pinned butterflies.

But old photo albums still show us,
Menacing,
Grinning diabolically,
Grade school soldiers dressed for the kill,
Doing our all to make the kitchen cupboards
Safe for Mother.

—Gene Fehler

Writing Opportunity

The first line of this poem begins with an action. Choose your own action and use it to begin a poem. Let one detail lead to another, until you've written your own poem about something that might or might not have actually happened to you.

Protector

Emerald, pencil thin,
the snake encircled his neck.
Before he could say "harmless,"
she screamed of fangs and poison venom
as if screams would save her son.
The snake unclasped itself,
slid to his shoulder.
He lifted it off.
"It's just a green snake," he said.
"Less dangerous than a red ant."

Maybe so. But that night
she filled the terrarium with water
and sealed the snake inside.
She would do the same with ants
if it came to that.

—Gene Fehler

A Word from the Poet

❝ Most poems fall somewhere between being all truth and all lies. 'Protector' begins with truth and ends in a lie. When my son Andy was in about seventh grade, he did walk into our house with a snake wrapped around his neck. And my wife did not like the spectacle. That much is true. The rest I made up. ❞

Writing Opportunity

Identify a moment from your personal experience, and begin a poem with details of what actually happened. Then complete the poem by telling lies! Invent details that will take the poem in a different direction—tell a different story, present a more dramatic situation, create some irony, or evoke a different mood than what was felt in your original experience.

CHAPTER TWO

Taking a Closer Look

Observing Your World

Imagine that you are riding down a country road, watching the trees rush past. Some people might just see a blur of green. But when you write poetry, you are challenged to see things in ways that are different from how most people view them.

As a poet, you need to catch a sharper image of the trees. You might see what kind of trees they are; you might notice their shapes or the size and condition of their trunks or branches; you might notice the range of shading in the color of their leaves; and you might notice birds nesting among the trees or squirrels scurrying among their branches. The most common senses used in writing poetry are touch and sight. But we also have to be aware of smells, tastes, and sounds.

Many poems are pieces of writing in which the author gives us a closer look and a closer listen to the world around us. As poets learn to study commonplace objects, places, or actions, they discover material for poems. They use their writing to share observations with their readers. Poets can craft the language in their poems to:

- compare objects.

- suggest how they feel about an object, place, or person.

- use strong sensory images (sight, sound, taste, touch, smell) to help readers share their perceptions of an object or a place.

- create a mood.

Ideas Are All Around Us

Always keep your eyes open and your mind receptive to new ideas as you observe the world around you, even at home. It might be fun to write poems about how we feel about our pets. But an even greater source for poetry is the countless things we see our pets do. Some kinds of pets can roam farther and perform a greater variety of tasks. But even a goldfish can inspire great poetry, if you really look, really observe its every move, every glimmer of light on its scales, every bubble from its mouth, and every trip it takes across the bottom of the aquarium.

Remember that poems need not always be profound or difficult. All they have to be is honest or imaginative reflections of what we see and feel.

Poetic Principle

Poems challenge you to see the world in ways that are different from how most people view it.

Writing from Your Heart

Writing poems demands that you observe closely with all your senses—sight, hearing, touch, taste, and smell. But you must also observe with your heart. Any time you feel emotion, a poem is possible. How you feel is essential; it is what shapes a poem in form and language. It also dictates the content of your poetry.

A poem can be a new way to let people know what's going on inside your mind. When someone reads your poem, he or she should be able to discover how you feel about something without having you explain. Readers should be left with a sense of how you (or the narrator in your poem) feel. When you read "A Dog at Roadside Studying Traffic Patterns on Busy Highway 40" (page 37) or "Phone Call to My Dog Poppins" (page 38), you soon discover how the narrator, or poet, feels about these two dogs and these situations.

If you feel strongly about something, write about it. But caring won't in itself make your poem good. The success of a poem depends not on how much emotion you felt when writing it, but on how much emotion the reader feels when reading it.

 ## Surprising Senses

Sometimes poets concentrate on one sense and develop their poems around it. I focused on my sense of hearing to write about sounds in "Thunder" (page 71), "Fingernail Clippers" (page 42), and "Trimming One's Nails in Public Places" (page 43).

But you can also create added surprises and freshness in your poetry by using unexpected senses. Consider the senses that come to mind when you think of ice cream. Taste? Touch? Sight? Take a moment to enjoy "The Sound of Ice Cream" (page 41) and its surprising images.

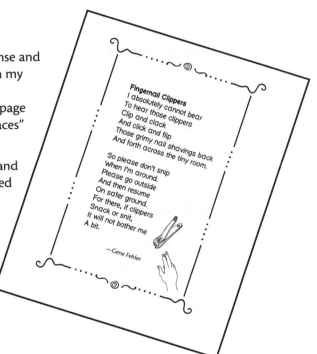

Fingernail Clippers

I absolutely cannot bear
To hear those clippers
Clip and clack
And click and flip
Those grimy nail shavings back
And forth across the tiny room.

So please don't snip
When I'm around.
Please go outside
And then resume
On safer ground.
For there, if clippers
Snack or snit,
It will not bother me
A bit.

—Gene Fehler

Poetic Principle

Any time you feel emotion, a poem is possible.

Observation and Haiku

While observation is important for all poetry, the Japanese form called *haiku* depends upon it. Traditionally, this type of poem has three lines of words totaling 17 syllables—five in the first line, seven in the second, and five in the third. Haiku often shows a moment in time, creates a mood, and presents a portrait of a scene in nature. Many modern poets now write haiku that have fewer than 17 syllables and do not restrict themselves to the 5–7–5 format. Yet the intent remains the same—to stir the reader's emotions with a vivid snapshot of a moment in time.

Consider the following haiku:

full moon frosty-ringed
painting the meadow's canvas
with charcoal shadows

This poem has a 5–7–5 syllable pattern. It stirs something in the mind or heart of the reader—an emotion, a recognition of some moment that is in some way identifiable.

A close relation to the haiku that uses the same form is the *senryu*. The basic difference is that the senryu often deals with human nature and is more likely to use humor than a haiku. Examine the following baseball-based haiku/senryu:

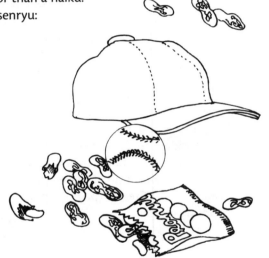

sky of rain diamonds
flung beneath a bank of lights:
damp jeweled splendor

summer afternoons,
breathing the infield dust,
smiling

in summer bleachers
peanut shells
crunch beneath my shoes

autumn wraps baseball
in dreams
to keep us warm all winter

—Gene Fehler

P̲o̤e̤t̲i̤c̲ P̲r̈i̇n̈c̲i̤p̲l̲e̲

Writing poems demands that you observe closely
with all your senses.

The Cinquain

The *cinquain* also has a specific form and is useful for recording observations. The cinquain has 22 syllables that are divided 2–4–6–8–2 among five lines. Here are two examples of cinquains that capture the poet's observations.

> bonecold
> autumn shadows
> catch flights of falling leaves
> cast out by thin branches' final
> shiver

> backyards
> of first graders
> sprinkled with fireflies
> capture shouts to be remembered
> someday

—Gene Fehler

And Now for Some Poems

The remainder of this chapter presents poems that evolved from my observations of the world around me. Some poems describe natural places, while others detail man-made locations; some mention events; others deal with people and animals. I have used all my senses to capture and portray my observations for my readers. Imagination and emotions are strongly reflected in my writing.

Once again, these poems include one or more writing opportunities to encourage you to explore and share your observations and emotions.

Poetic Principle

A poem is not significant because of any inherent drama
in what it describes,
but because the poet's vision gives it significance.

66 'Jungle Warfare' describes what I saw in my family's bathroom sink one morning after one of my sons had finished brushing his teeth.

"While this is essentially a free verse poem, random rhyme is still possible. You can see this in *pain* and *rain*. As poets, we simply have to determine whether we feel such rhyme adds to or detracts from each poem. And alas, there are no easy ways to know. Either it sounds right or it doesn't. 99

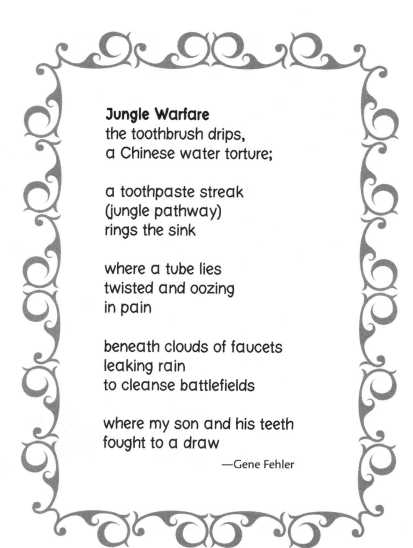

Jungle Warfare
the toothbrush drips,
a Chinese water torture;

a toothpaste streak
(jungle pathway)
rings the sink

where a tube lies
twisted and oozing
in pain

beneath clouds of faucets
leaking rain
to cleanse battlefields

where my son and his teeth
fought to a draw
—Gene Fehler

Writing Opportunity

Look closely at something in your house that you have seen thousands of times before. Try to see something new about it. Look at it with completely fresh eyes, as if you are seeing it for the first time. What do you see? Use words to capture your observations.

Fielder's Mitt
On the shelf my mitt,
stiff from winter's bench-
warming cold,
waits for spring,
for mud-scuffed balls
slapping past, taunting
"Catch me if you can!"
a challenge
that thaws my mitt
for a chase
through any mud-
warmed ballpark
in suddenly
spring.

—Gene Fehler

Writing Opportunity

When you wake up in the morning, what is the first thing you see? Describe it in a poem. How do you feel about it?

❝ I looked at a beach and a meadow and made a list of things I saw at each place. I decided to use rhyme in showing these things to the reader.

"In 'The Beach' I used rhymed couplets; in 'The Meadow' I rhymed the second, fourth, and sixth lines. I also used lots of alliteration to make these poems fun to read. Look for *shadowy/shore, seashell/seagull, white wings, silvery sliver, sweet summer, bluebonnets/ bees, snake slithers/ summer's, green grasses,* and *caterpillars crawl.*

"Finally, I took special care to make the rhythm smooth, natural, and flowing. If I succeeded, the reader will enjoy listening to the poems not only for the pictures they create, but also for how they sound.❞

The Beach
The shadowy things that I see on the shore
Might be starfish or crabs or a large albacore.
Or a lobster or seashell or seagull's white wings,
Which at nighttime are dark like all shadowy things.
And beyond them, a whale—or maybe sand dune
Beneath the curved silvery sliver of moon.

—Gene Fehler

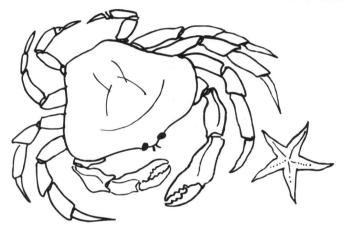

The Meadow
Butterflies flutter in sweet summer meadows
Where daisies and bluebonnets wait for the bees.
A garter snake slithers through summer's green grasses,
And brown caterpillars crawl onto my knees.
The day-games of nature begin, and two night owls
Awaken and offer to be referees.

—Gene Fehler

Writing Opportunity

Write a poem about a place, describing to the reader many of the things you see there. You might try to use couplets (two consecutive rhymed lines), as in "The Beach." Or you might imitate the rhyme scheme of "The Meadow" (ABCBDB: the first, third, and fifth lines do not rhyme; but the second, fourth, and sixth do).

Rain Out

On the dugout
roof
raindrops thud
and laugh—
they're mocking
me

as infield
rivers
wash my
baseball dreams
far out to
sea.

❝ These poems take a
close look at three places
that are important to me.
See if you can find the
metaphors and personifica-
tion I've used to make these
places seem more real. ❞

Alchemy

I zip open my gym bag,
watch the coming game leak out.
spreading itself on the locker room bench
like sweat.
Around the room more bags zip open;
twelve different games
run over themselves.
Coach moves among us,
a modern alchemist mixing tonight's gold.

Cobwebbed Bedroom Corners

cobwebbed
bedroom corners:
strands of cotton candy
in a carnival of sleep-spun
nightmares

—Gene Fehler

Writing Opportunity

Use random rhyme or the
cinquain form to write about a
place that is important to you. Be
sure to show the reader some of the
sights, sounds, and smells of the
place. Try to use personification or
metaphors in your poem.

66 Years ago I stood outside the Haish Memorial Library in DeKalb, Illinois. As I waited for it to open, I thought about the names carved into the stone building. I jotted notes on a notepad, wrote down the names, and admired the hedges. Days later, after several drafts, the poem moved from free verse to rhyme. **99**

The Haish Memorial Library
Hedges, low and green, fresh-clipped
Encircle bright, book-blooming rooms.
I wonder if the hand that grooms
Those hedges is the same that chipped
That precious permanence in stone
That tells us we are not alone.
The carved words are too large, too strong
To be erased by all the wrong
That shouts across the modern face
Of time. The ultimate disgrace,
Big Brother, cannot hush the shout
From names carved on the building's wall:
Socrates, Homer, Shakespeare—all
Help us to live and love and think.
They tell us we can live without
The modern world's transparent ink.

—Gene Fehler

Writing Opportunity

Imagine yourself standing outside a building, and write a poem about what you see or how you feel. Consider one or more of the following questions: *What is the building? Why are you there? What does it look like? What makes the building so special?*

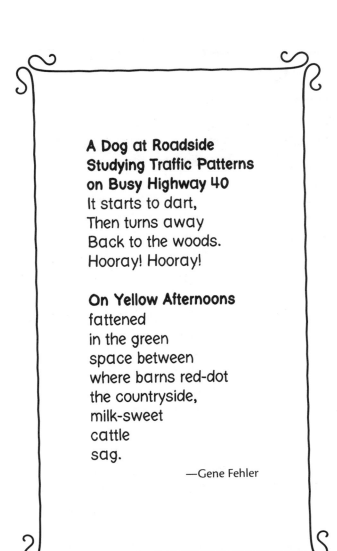

**A Dog at Roadside
Studying Traffic Patterns
on Busy Highway 40**
It starts to dart,
Then turns away
Back to the woods.
Hooray! Hooray!

On Yellow Afternoons
fattened
in the green
space between
where barns red-dot
the countryside,
milk-sweet
cattle
sag.

—Gene Fehler

❝ These two short poems came about as a result of things I observed while driving down the highway. The first poem was a moment of high drama to me. I saw a dog that I thought was preparing to commit suicide by dashing in front of some fast-moving cars. The second poem resulted from the simple sight on a yellow afternoon of a cow grazing.

"In both poems I tried to use the best form and words to capture the moment. One poem ended up as a rhymed poem, the other free verse.❞

Writing Opportunity

Write a poem of any length and form about something you have actually observed from a car or bus window. Write exactly what you see, but try to use language and form that make the observation seem new, fresh, and interesting to the reader.

Phone Call to My Dog Poppins

When she saw me pack to leave on a five-day trip,
she jumped onto my bed, wagging her tail,
begging for me to take her with me.

When I phoned home two days later,
my wife told me Poppins had barely moved,
just lay listless, sad eyes half open.
Then my wife held the phone to Poppins' ear
as I said, "I love you, Poppins. I'll be home soon."

"Her tail's going a mile a minute," my wife said.
"She's watching the door. She thinks you're home."

Three days later, when I entered our house for real,
I bent down and Poppins greeted me with a week's
worth of kisses, wet tongue showing her joy.

I still wonder if it was a thought that stopped her
in the middle of her frenzied welcome,
that made her turn and trot to her bed and lie silent.
Perhaps she meant to punish me, or maybe
was moved by sudden shame at having given her love
so freely, so fully to someone as fickle as I,
someone so mean as to not take her with me,
so thoughtless as to tease her with phone calls
when all she knows of phones
is that they have never rubbed her tummy,
have never thrown a ball to her in the backyard.

All she knows of phones is that they are hard,
lifeless things that do not have faces to kiss.

—Gene Fehler

Writing Opportunity

Write about a time a pet (it might belong to you or someone else) seemed excited to see you or bored or angry with you. What do you think you did to cause that reaction?

Fullcourt Magic

The ball bounces once,
twice.
I scoop it up with my right hand,
take three dribbles,
give a head fake to the right,
flip a behind-the-back pass to Russell
breaking for the basket
between two defenders
running step for step with him
as smoothly and tightly
as two more sets of skin.

Sprinting full speed,
he gathers the pass,
spins in mid-air
and skips the ball off the glass.
It kisses net
and drops through to the court.

I can almost imagine
the ball's smile
as it waits for a new set of hands
to grasp it,
to shape it
into another piece of fullcourt magic.

—Gene Fehler

❝ Have you ever witnessed an athletic achievement that amazed or excited you? Perhaps it was a crucial point in a tennis match, a soccer game, or a routine on the ice.

"Instant replay gives us something fans 30 years ago didn't have—a chance to appreciate over and over the beauty of a single moment in sports. Anyone who has ever watched basketball has seen the kind of moment described in this poem; all I tried to do was to become a camera and record each movement. **❞**

Writing Opportunity

Write a poem in which you describe a particular sports moment. Observe the moment closely. Recapture as specifically as possible the details of that brief period of time. Show the moment; don't simply tell about it.

The Clothesline in the Backyard

Clothes clap in the stiff wind roaring
from the west across the flatlands of Kansas.
Shirts wave toward wheat fields
while inside the farmhouse a woman
sits by her husband's bed, holds his hand.
With a damp cloth she soothes his face.
She reminds him of the day they danced
that evening twenty-eight years ago
at the high school dance, the first time
she really noticed him enough to look beyond
his too-large ears and goofy grin. His large hands
were gentle. His eyes showed a warmth
that surprised her. She brushes his still dark hair
from his forehead, wipes her tears from his cheek.
Passing hours turn voices into whispers.
Outside the window, light fades.
The wind stops. Along the clothesline,
faded work clothes hang limp.

—Gene Fehler

Writing Opportunity

Notice how "The Clothesline in the Backyard" begins with things—clothes. I then picture the clothes, describing where they are and what they are doing. I add actions, places, people, and time to build the poem.

Choose your own object or thing and use it to develop a poem of your own.

The Sound of Ice Cream
Joey bought an ice-cream cone
    And listened to it melt.
It was a sad and lonely sound,
    And warmer than it felt.

It sounded much like winter
    When the grass is dead and gone,
And frozen feet are crunching on
    Vanilla ice-cream lawn.

It felt as warm as August
    When taste buds start to scream,
Then listen to their echo:
    "I really love ice cream!"

Joey started licking it,
    And soon it disappeared.
He listened for his taste buds
    And giggled when they cheered.

—Gene Fehler

66 Don't look for anything profound in this poem. It is basically nonsense, intended mainly to create a mood or a surprise by using an unexpected sense—hearing. If nothing else, try to find one thing you might like in it—perhaps the rhymes, maybe the personification of the taste buds, or even the winter snow described as a *vanilla ice-cream lawn.* Maybe you can share in the giggle of the taste buds. **99**

Writing Opportunity

Write a poem in which you use a surprising sense. For example, you might write about the sound or smell of a cactus, the weight of piano notes floating above the piano, the taste of a summer's breeze as you jog around the block, or someone's smile or frown touching you.

❝ My wife Polly has a particularly strong aversion to the sound of fingernails or toenails being clipped. If she happens to find herself in a room where someone is trimming lengthy nails, her reaction is not as calm as the first poem might suggest. In 'Fingernail Clippers,' I put myself in Polly's place and described her feelings. In 'Trimming One's Nails in Public Places', I do the same but show more clearly my wife's feelings about the act. ❞

Fingernail Clippers
I absolutely cannot bear
To hear those clippers
Clip and clack
And click and flip
Those grimy nail shavings back
And forth across the tiny room.

So please don't snip
When I'm around.
Please go outside
And then resume
On safer ground.
For there, if clippers
Snack or snit,
It will not bother me
A bit.

—Gene Fehler

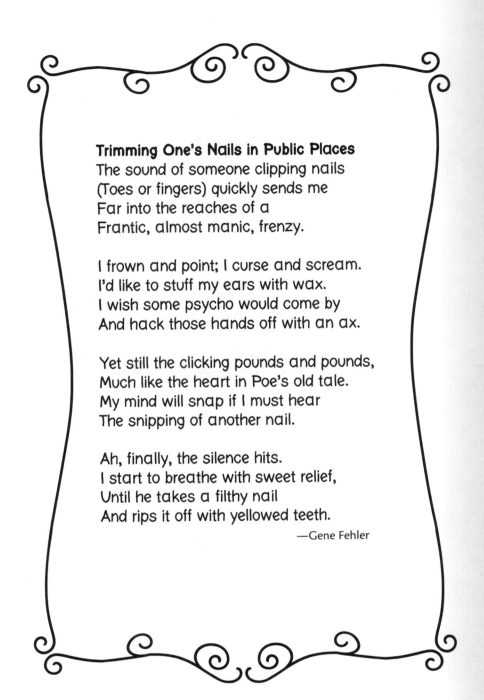

Trimming One's Nails in Public Places

The sound of someone clipping nails
(Toes or fingers) quickly sends me
Far into the reaches of a
Frantic, almost manic, frenzy.

I frown and point; I curse and scream.
I'd like to stuff my ears with wax.
I wish some psycho would come by
And hack those hands off with an ax.

Yet still the clicking pounds and pounds,
Much like the heart in Poe's old tale.
My mind will snap if I must hear
The snipping of another nail.

Ah, finally, the silence hits.
I start to breathe with sweet relief,
Until he takes a filthy nail
And rips it off with yellowed teeth.

—Gene Fehler

Writing Opportunity

Make a list of several things with distinctive sounds or of places or actions that generate particular sounds. Write a poem in which the sense of sound is key to your poem.

Write a poem about the most unpleasant or pleasant sound you have ever heard.

A child of twilight:
his icy mood lies melting
on the gray pier.

"Yet individual images and rough drafts always offer the possibility of expansion. I decided I wanted to say even more about that child, so I started accumulating a list of other observations. I wanted to include additional sights and sounds that affected his mood, and perhaps the reader's as well. **99**

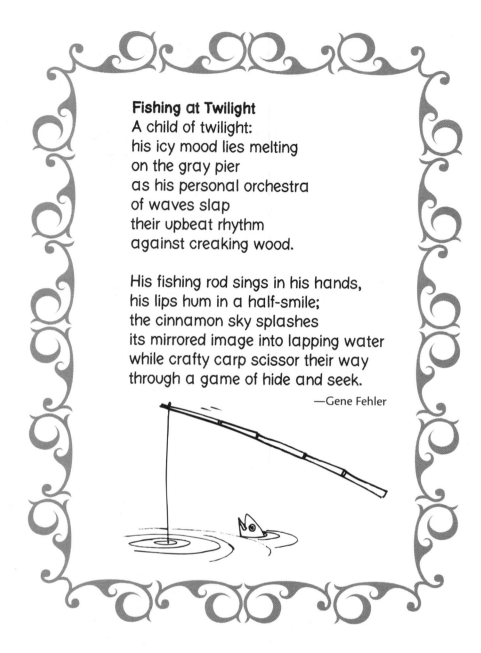

Fishing at Twilight
A child of twilight:
his icy mood lies melting
on the gray pier
as his personal orchestra
of waves slap
their upbeat rhythm
against creaking wood.

His fishing rod sings in his hands,
his lips hum in a half-smile;
the cinnamon sky splashes
its mirrored image into lapping water
while crafty carp scissor their way
through a game of hide and seek.

—Gene Fehler

Writing Opportunity

Write your own haiku. First, try to fit your observation of a moment into the 5–7–5 syllable framework. Then, simply try to write a short three-line observation of some moment without worrying about syllable count.

Write several haiku. Then take one and expand it into a longer poem. What details can you add to give the reader an even sharper or more complete picture of the place, time, person, or action depicted?

CHAPTER THREE

Learning to Enjoy Poetry

Can There Be Fun in Poetry?

From nursery rhymes to advertising jingles to more serious verse, poetry can be fun! And we are not just talking about the kind of poetry that makes us laugh; sad or contemplative poetry can be fun too. We can enjoy not only the humor or drama in a poem, but also its pleasing sounds, clever use of language, ironies, and well-crafted structure. And if the only fun we can find in a poem is that it makes us laugh—well, that's a good place to start. After all, there are no wrong reasons to enjoy poetry!

As poets, our goal should be to let readers of all ages see how much fun poetry can be. As readers, it doesn't matter whether we understand a poem in the same way someone else does. Nor is it important for us to identify every technique used by a poet. We should simply try to find at least one thing to enjoy in each poem we read. Then we might want to read it a second or a third time to make additional discoveries.

Take a moment to enjoy this silly poem about homework. It serves no purpose except to provide humor for its writer and readers.

The Last Time I Did Homework

Last month I did some homework,
    And then my puppy ate it.
He growled at me, so it was clear
    That even puppies hate it.

I told my teacher that my puppy
    Thinks it's mighty cruel:
That awful-tasting homework
    We're asked to learn for school.

She said to bring my puppy in
    The next day, and no later.
But when the two came face to face,
    My foolish puppy ate her.

—Gene Fehler

Poetic Principle

Poetry is not a punishment, but a pleasure.

 **Limericks**

One form of poetry that can be fun is the *limerick*, a five-line verse form. A limerick gives us the chance to be silly while experimenting with rhyme and rhythm. The first, second, and fifth lines of a limerick rhyme with each other; and then the third line rhymes with the fourth. The basic rhythm of a limerick is usually:

      da-da-DA da-da-DA da-da-DA,

      da-da-DA da-da-DA da-da-DA.

         da-da-DA da-da-DA,

         da-da-DA da-da-DA,

      da-da-DA da-da-DA da-da-DA.

Remember these key points about limericks:

■ Limericks are usually silly, but you should still work as hard on them as you would other forms of poetry.

■ Even though you may begin with an illogical premise (e.g., *A worm waved to me from the grass*), you need to carry the story to a logical conclusion.

■ Try to use the same elements that you use in more serious forms of poetry (e.g., sound devices, strong verbs, imaginative comparisons, strong images, irony).

■ If none of your rhymed words seems to fit, you might change the first line, giving yourself a different end word to work with.

Here are two silly limericks to share with a friend. Look for others on page 53.

A guy threw a pie in my face
And it splattered all over the place.
    When I asked, "Why do that?"
    He replied with a splat
From another pie in the same place.

Though the foot that is there in my shoe
Smells bad, there's not much I can do.
    I wash eight times a day,
    Scrub the skin half away,
But it still smells no better than you.

—Gene Fehler

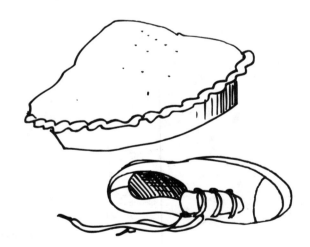

Poetic Principle

Try to find at least one thing to enjoy in each poem you read.

How Can You Make Poetry Fun?

Some people think poetry is boring. Perhaps they feel that some poems are too long, or they cannot understand what other ones are about. They might be puzzled because a poem doesn't rhyme or uses words they do not know. So what can you do to make poetry more fun for yourself and others?

Explore Shorter Poems

Many top poetry magazines publish quality poetry (mainly free verse) over a hundred lines long. These poems are almost always written by established poets who have mastered their craft, who are skilled in the use of imagery, metaphor, and symbolism. These are poets who have learned how to build a long poem without wasting words. However, unless and until you've reached that level, it's better to concentrate on tightening your poems by thinking "short" rather than "long." And shorter poems, especially by beginning poets, are more publishable than long ones.

What are the advantages of shorter poems?

- Readers are less intimidated.

- Poets must tighten their language.

- Poets are less likely to fall into the trap of "over writing."

- If a poet really doesn't like his or her poem, then he or she hasn't wasted too much time!

Understand the Words

If you don't understand a key word in a poem, the impact of the entire poem will likely be deflated like a punctured tire or balloon. This problem is easily solved for a reader—get a dictionary. However, the poet has a responsibility too. In a good poem, every word should be carefully chosen, and the poet should try to use the best possible words in the best possible order.

Sometimes the simplest word will be the most effective one. Beginning poets often think that big, unfamiliar words sound impressive. But if you use too many words that are unfamiliar to your reader, you will probably weaken rather than strengthen your poem. Your task as a poet is not to hopelessly confuse the reader; it is to present your subject as intensely, clearly, and powerfully as possible.

Poetic Principle

Short poems are often more publishable than long ones.

Understand the Poem

To paraphrase poet Marianne Moore, we do not admire what we cannot understand. If a poem puzzles you, then examine it more carefully. You should:

- look up the meanings of any unfamiliar words (see page 47).

- find out what is really happening in the poem. Who are the people? Is the poet trying to describe a scene? What physical action is taking place?

- read the poem several times, taking a close look at each line and image. Perhaps the third or fourth (or tenth) reading will suggest an idea that was not apparent in earlier readings. If you're still lost after reading the poem several times, then read it without worrying what it's about. Try to enjoy its sounds, its craft, any unusual use of language, or any striking images. Sometimes readers worry too much about what a poem "means."

You can increase your understanding and appreciation of a poem by looking at what other knowledgeable readers of poetry have to say. Don't get frustrated if they see things in a poem that you don't notice. They may have had an experience similar to that of the poet, have had more experience reading poetry, or be seeing something totally different from what the poet intended.

Remember that any time several people try to judge which of two poems is better, there is seldom unanimous agreement. Begin by forming your own emotional and intellectual reaction to a poem. What it means to you—and what it does for you—are more important than what it means or does for someone else. In short, a poem is a personal communication between you and the poet.

 ## Be Open to New Experiences

You might understand the experience presented in the poem, yet still be bored by it because the poet's experience is foreign to your own. Is this the fault of the reader or the poet? Perhaps a bit of both.

As a reader, you should be open to reading about new experiences. As a poet, you must share the experience as concretely as possible so the reader sees and feels (and hears, tastes, and smells) all that you see and feel (and hear, taste, and smell).

Poetic Principle

We do not admire what we cannot understand.

Enjoy Different Forms of Poetry

If you have read only rhymed poems, you might have a hard time appreciating free verse poetry. If you've mainly read straightforward and easy-to-understand poems, you might not feel comfortable with ones that are highly symbolic or have implied ideas.

Most of us feel uncomfortable with the unfamiliar. We can only become familiar with poetry by reading it. Read all kinds—rhymed, unrhymed, imagistic, symbolic, implicit, explicit—poems that challenge the senses, the emotions, and the intellect. Go to a library and look for poetry books with collections of rhymed and unrhymed poems. And enjoy reading them!

Accept the fact that poems can be simple or complex and can often sound more like prose than we might expect. Poems can express any emotion, deal with an unlimited range of topics, and take widely divergent forms. Just look at the many different types of poems in this book!

 ## Know Poetic Devices

Once in a while, most people come up with an idea that they believe would make a great book, screenplay, or poem. But almost all of them don't know how to transfer their idea to a well-crafted written form.

While this book does not go into a detailed study of poetic devices, many of them will be mentioned. Devices such as *metaphors*, *hyperbole*, and *irony* are the essence of poetry. Try to familiarize yourself with as many poetic devices as you can. Study the techniques used by other writers—not to imitate their personal styles but to examine some of the elements that make their writing good reading. Only through an understanding of all the poet's tools can you fully appreciate poetry. And only by knowing these tools can you effectively develop your own style and potential as a poet and reader of poetry.

Poetic Principle

Remember that the same poem can mean something totally different to each reader.

An Introduction to Style

Style encompasses the way poets present and express their ideas. It is a reflection of his or her personality; vision; and ways of feeling, thinking, and observing. Each person's writing displays some unique qualities unless he or she is imitating a specific poet.

The very best writers are those who do not sound like anyone else; they sound like themselves. If we read a Robert Frost poem, we are likely to say, "That sounds like Robert Frost!" The same can be said of most great poets. They have their own individual ways of seeing, speaking, and using form and language patterns.

Some poets rely heavily on similes and metaphors; others use personification or irony. Some writers are pessimistic and despairing, their dark vision of the world showing through in what they write. Other poets are hopeful and optimistic, looking at the world with light, sparkling wit. They make the reader feel good with each line.

In many poems, writers pretend to be someone else. While pretending is certainly an important technique for creating characters and stories, keep in mind that personal style is much like a fingerprint; it's hard to hide who you really are, and you often have your best results when you don't try to hide your style.

In order to do your best work, you must learn to write by writing as much as you can. And you must be yourself as you write, developing personal style— your own individual voice that rings true. Don't try to sound exactly like your favorite writers. They have already mastered their voices; you will only sound like a weak imitation.

Expectation and Surprise

An important aspect of style is the balancing of expectation and surprise. A poet often achieves a striking effect by surprising the reader with a comparison, image, rhyme, or idea that is totally unexpected. Without surprises, most writing wouldn't make for interesting reading. Look for surprises in many of the poems in this book, including "The Shot Blocker" (page 57) and "Rats" (page 59). Remember that when we write, we don't have to know how our poems will end. Sometimes we write to discover the endings; we don't always have to know them in advance.

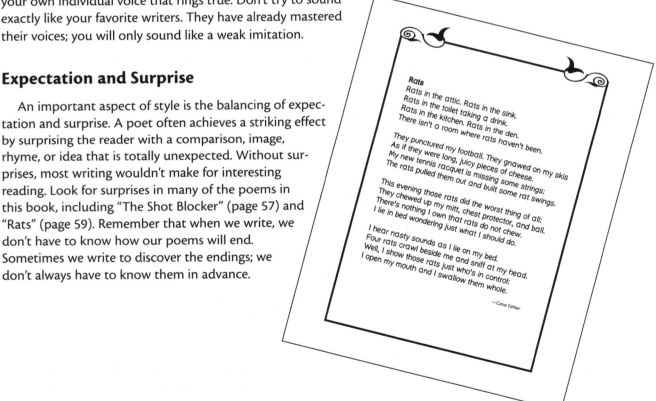

Rats

Rats in the attic. Rats in the sink.
Rats in the toilet taking a drink.
Rats in the kitchen. Rats in the den.
There isn't a room where rats haven't been.

They punctured my football. They gnawed on my skis
As if they were long, juicy pieces of cheese.
My new tennis racquet is missing some strings:
The rats pulled them out and built some rat swings.

This evening those rats did the worst thing of all:
They chewed up my mitt, chest protector, and ball.
There's nothing I own that rats do not chew.
I lie in bed wondering just what I should do.

I hear nasty sounds as I lie on my bed.
Four rats crawl beside me and sniff at my head.
Well, I show those rats just who's in control:
I open my mouth and I swallow them whole.

—Gene Fehler

Poetic Principle

Without surprises, most writing wouldn't make
for interesting reading.

Personification, Similes, and Metaphors

Similes and metaphors are among the most widely used and effective poetic devices. They give the reader a fresh new way of looking at something.

A *simile* is an implied comparison between two dissimilar things. It suggests that two things are really alike in some way even though we usually think of them as totally different. A simile doesn't make an actual comparison; it says that one thing is *like* or *as* something else. For example: *Life is like a bowl of cherries.*

A *metaphor* is an actual comparison between two dissimilar things; it says that one thing *is* another. A metaphor is a simile without the connective words *like* or *as*. For example: *Life is a bowl of cherries.*

Personification is a device in which a thing, animal, or abstract idea (such as *truth* or *nature*) is given human qualities or attributes. For example: *The bowl of cherries began to giggle.*

Look for these devices in many poems in this book, such as "Ice-Skating on Weak Ankles" (page 60), "My Pitching Lullaby" (page 61), and "The Snow and the Heat" (page 62).

Sound Devices

Pleasing sound devices can make a poem fun to read. Poets often use *alliteration*, a succession of words that have the same beginning letter. They might include words beginning with letters like *s*, *l*, or *w* to suggest soft sounds or quiet moods; and words with letters like *g* and *k* to suggest harsher sounds and more intense emotions. Discover the alliteration in poems such as "Tent Painter" and "K-Things" (page 63).

Poets also use or create phrases with words that seem to imitate sounds (*onomatopoeia*). Enjoy the many "sound" words in "My Sports Onomatopoeia" (page 64).

And Now for Some Poems

The remainder of this chapter presents poems and writing opportunities that demonstrate quite simply that poetry is fun and enjoyable. Many of the poems illustrate that we can appreciate a poem for our own reasons and that poetry often suggests more questions than answers. These poems also demonstrate various poetic devices and provide opportunities for us to incorporate them into our writing.

Poetic Principle

Accept whatever brings you pleasure in a poem;
there will be time later to study it on a more analytical level
(if you wish).

66 When my son Tim was in fourth grade, we decided to collaborate on some limericks together. We used these guidelines:

■ Write an eight- or nine-syllable line.

■ The line can be about any subject.

■ The line doesn't have to be a complete sentence.

■ The line can be absurd or nonsensical.

"Here are some of our first lines:

The cat ate the bird for dessert

A worm waved to me from the grass

My baseball-dumb mother had heard

The python climbed up in the tree

A monster gazed down at his plate

When bending to sniff at the rose

A man swam a race with an eel

"What was really fun for us was that most of our first lines were written without any idea of what was to follow. Then we took turns completing them as limericks (see page 53). 99

Writing Opportunity

Look at the beginning lines for limericks on the left. Experiment with some of them and try to write second lines. Then see if you can complete some of the limericks.

Read the limericks written by me and my son. Did you approach any of yours in the same way? Probably not. That's the beauty of poetry; we all have different visions.

Try writing your own first lines. Choose one line and use it to write your own complete limerick.

Limericks

The cat ate the bird for dessert.
It swallowed and asked, "Does it hurt?"
    The bird said, "Not really.
    But don't you feel silly?
You swallowed my ten dollar shirt."

A worm waved to me from the grass.
He had learned how to in etiquette class.
    Now a day can't go by
    When that worm doesn't try
To tip his top hat when I pass.

My baseball-dumb mother had heard
I like to play second and third.
    "Though it's only a game,"
    My mom muttered in shame,
"To want less than first is absurd!"

The python climbed up in the tree.
Where it crawled to, I couldn't quite see.
    So I stood there in fear
    Hoping I wouldn't hear
Something slither down softly on me.

A monster gazed down at his plate.
He started to nibble, and ate
    Half a finger and toe.
    Then his wife told him, "Oh!
We didn't say grace; you must wait!"

When bending to sniff at the rose,
A bumblebee flew on her nose.
    The bee wouldn't sting
    That long, ugly thing
That he thought was a green garden hose.

A man swam a race with an eel,
With a walrus, a shark, and a seal.
    The shark was the winner,
    So he had for his dinner
The losers, who made quite a meal.

—Gene Fehler

66 I didn't really try to write poetry until I was in my thirties. Once I did start writing, I spent two years collecting rejection slips from publishers before I realized the error of my ways—my poems were at least twice as long as they should have been. Once I started to cut my poems down to 30 or 20 (or fewer) lines, I started getting poems regularly published in magazines.

"In 'Boy Visiting Father,' I tried to cut unnecessary words as I told my story. Perhaps you will see still other words in this poem that could be cut. However, take a look at the second poem on this page to see that you can write a poem so short that the title is longer! 99

Boy Visiting Father
fog.
snow.
Greyhound bus.

a woman
in a green coat
by the curb,

waving
as the bus
turns the corner,

waving
across silent tire marks
in the slush

**The Day I Drew a Girl as My Opponent
in My First and Only School Wrestling Match**
she pinned me flat against the mat.
and that was that.

—Gene Fehler

Writing Opportunity

Write a free verse poem of any length and form in which you describe something you have observed. Don't pass judgment or draw any conclusions—merely show the reader what you see.

Once you have written your rough draft, start cutting words. Try to keep your poem as short as possible. "Boy Visiting Father" is 28 words long. Try to write some poems that are no longer than this one.

© Good Apple GA13062

Tribute to Captain Kirk

Oh, Captain Kirk, this is for you,
you who have been nailed on the cross-
references of our memory banks,
you who have taught us all we know
of the universe and cosmos and planetoids
and astrals and the extraterrestrial,
you who have taken us aliens with you
from the mundane hours of our lives
into the nanoseconds and millennia and eons
when your transmutation from a chrysalid
to an eidolon has left us in the whirl
of your maelstrom where infinity waits,
smiling, just around the galaxy.

—Gene Fehler

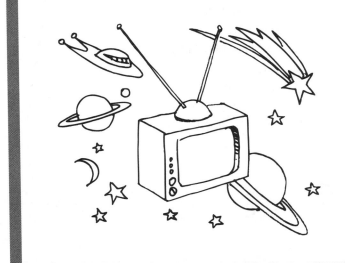

❝ I've received favorable comments about a poem I wrote about the fictional character Captain Kirk from the original *Star Trek* television series.

"Sometimes when I read this poem, I ask students if anyone can tell me what it means.

"Occasionally, a brave student will attempt to discuss its meaning, sometimes even coming up with something plausible. Then I tell them about the circumstances under which I wrote the poem.

"I had just completed reading a small collection of science-fiction poetry. I made a list of all the words I was unfamiliar with and decided to use them in a poem. 'Tribute to Captain Kirk' was the result of that experiment. I don't have any idea what the poem means; I was just trying to put unfamiliar words together in a way that seemed fairly logical. ❞

Writing Opportunity

Write a poem of any length or form in which you present information or feelings about a character from television or the movies—perhaps a "tribute" to that character.

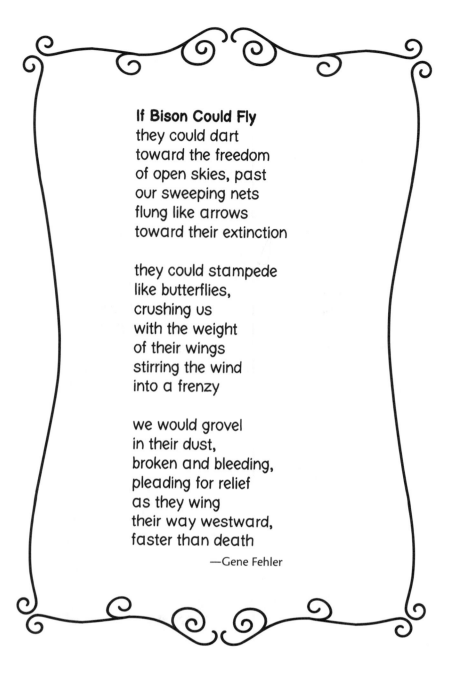

66 This poem is about bison. Or is it? Different readers have seen a wide range of ideas suggested by this poem. Should we limit it to a single idea? I hope not. Any idea the poem suggests to you is fine by me.

"By the way, my original title for this poem was 'If Buffalo Could Fly.' One of my young sons said, 'Dad, it sounds like your poem's going to be about Buffalo, New York. Why not change *buffalo* to *bison*?' Sometimes it pays to listen to critics, young or old. **99**

If Bison Could Fly
they could dart
toward the freedom
of open skies, past
our sweeping nets
flung like arrows
toward their extinction

they could stampede
like butterflies,
crushing us
with the weight
of their wings
stirring the wind
into a frenzy

we would grovel
in their dust,
broken and bleeding,
pleading for relief
as they wing
their way westward,
faster than death

—Gene Fehler

Writing Opportunity

Write a poem in which you begin your first line with the word *if*. Try to propose something that seems highly improbable (e.g., *If postage stamps could see; If mountain peaks could scratch the sky; If desks could fly*). Carry your poem out to its logical conclusion.

The Shot Blocker
I blocked his shot!
I blocked his shot!
The first blocked shot I ever got!

('Course, I'd have been much better off
if we'd played basketball, not golf.)

—Gene Fehler

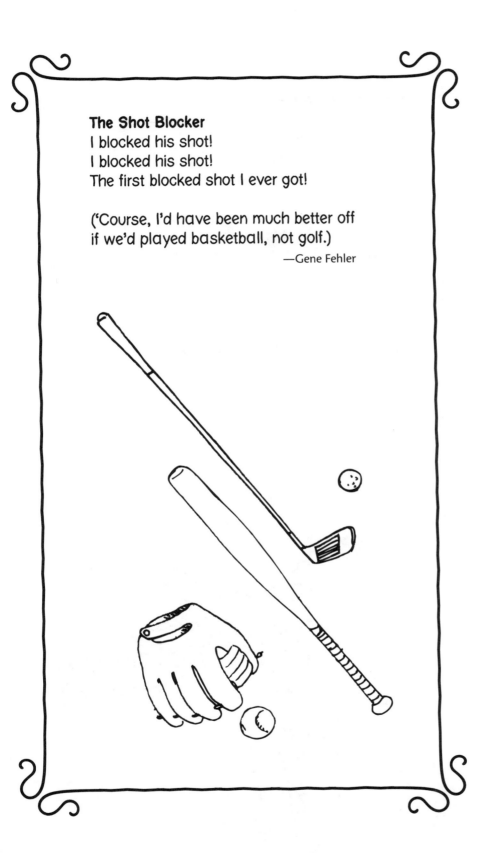

❝ I wrote this poem to experiment with using surprise endings.

"Whenever I read this poem out loud, I give the title and ask what sport my audience expects it to be about. People usually say basketball or soccer or hockey—but never golf! By the way, this actually happened to me on the golf course; a golf ball hit me on my arm. It wasn't fun. ❞

That Ump Makes Me So Mad!

That blind old ump behind the plate!—
    He's such a scary sight.
His eyes look like tomatoes;
    His teeth are long and white.

Just like a dragon, flames shoot out
    From both his ears and nose.
And he calls "strike" on everything
    The other pitcher throws

(Especially when I'm at bat,
    And oh, it makes me mad!)
But when he doesn't ump my games,
    I really love my dad.

—Gene Fehler

Rats

Rats in the attic. Rats in the sink.
Rats in the toilet taking a drink.
Rats in the kitchen. Rats in the den.
There isn't a room where rats haven't been.

They punctured my football. They gnawed on my skis
As if they were long, juicy pieces of cheese.
My new tennis racquet is missing some strings:
The rats pulled them out and built some rat swings.

This evening those rats did the worst thing of all:
They chewed up my mitt, chest protector, and ball.
There's nothing I own that rats do not chew.
I lie in bed wondering just what I should do.

I hear nasty sounds as I lie on my bed.
Four rats crawl beside me and sniff at my head.
Well, I show those rats just who's in control:
I open my mouth and I swallow them whole.

—Gene Fehler

66 I did not expect this poem to end this way. As I was writing it, I had no idea the narrator would swallow the rats. One line led into another and another. Before I knew it, I saw the narrator swallow the rats. Believe me, I was just as surprised as anyone! **99**

Writing Opportunity

Now, try your hand at writing a poem (free verse or rhymed) that has a surprise ending.

66 My wife Polly grew up in Hebron, Illinois and was a wonderful ice skater; I was not. Even though I grew up near the Mississippi River in northern Illinois and had plenty of ice to skate on, I didn't do much ice-skating. But I thought I had a good excuse.

"So, alas, this poem is all too true. 99

Ice-Skating on Weak Ankles
Legs wobble like noodles;
     The ice is unkind—
It flies up to meet me
     And whacks my behind.

A week on the pond
     And I'm covered with welts.
My bruised body yearns
     For the day the ice melts.
—Gene Fehler

Writing Opportunity

This poem begins with a simile: *Legs wobble like noodles.* Think of imaginative comparisons to complete the following lines with either a simile or metaphor.

Walking on hard snow sounds like . . .
Gnats swarm like . . .
The cloud is . . .
Words stick to the tongue like . . .
The ringing of the school bell . . .
Life on soap operas is . . .
The raw egg feels like . . .
His eyes are . . .
The moon is blazing like . . .
My alarm clock is . . .

Select an object of your own choosing and describe it in a fresh new way by using a simile or metaphor. Then use that object as the basis for a poem.

My Pitching Lullaby
The ball
starts its lullaby
in my pitching
hand

sings
all the way
into the
muffled darkness

of the
catcher's
pillowed
mitt.

—Gene Fehler

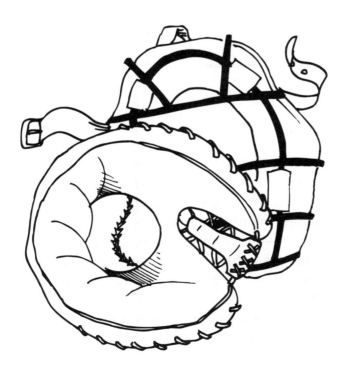

❝ I tend to write many poems about sports, especially baseball. Why? Because baseball has always been one of the biggest loves of my life, and I write about the things that move me.

"In 'My Pitching Lullaby,' I used personification to describe the act of successfully pitching a baseball to the catcher, from the pitcher's perspective. I've given the ball the ability to sing—in this instance, to sing the batter to sleep and strike him out.

"In 'The Snow and the Heat' (page 62), I used metaphor to describe the act of successfully hitting a baseball from the batter's perspective. The ball is snow; the bat is something producing enough heat to melt the snow to reshape it into what the batter, not the pitcher, wants.

"In 'My Pitching Lullaby' and 'The Snow and the Heat,' I had to decide what form to use for my completed poems. There's no right or wrong way. I decided to write them as long, skinny poems, with only one or two words on most of the lines. Was that the best way? I don't know. All I know is that they seemed to look good on the page. I usually retype free verse several ways to choose the form that looks best. **❞**

The Snow and the Heat
The pitcher's
leg
steps off the mountain;
he flings
snow from
the mountain's
peak.

I watch
from below.
The heat
from my bat
waits to
meet
the white
storm,

to send snow
back in a form
no one will
recognize,
or catch.

—Gene Fehler

Writing Opportunity

Write about an event in which you have participated—a play, concert, sports event, shopping excursion, classroom experience, or disagreement with someone. Write two poems—one from your perspective and the other from the perspective of someone else involved in the experience. Your poems should illustrate how the same experience can be viewed in completely different ways by two different people.

Tent Painter
Beneath the white whale
of unwalled tent,
she sketches strangers seated
stiff against the threat
of truth splashing in soft colors
behind her artist's easel.
They hope the scattering of lines
will shape their profiles
not as who her trained eyes see
but as who they wish to be:
a fantasy of cuteness,
of beauty bending
across the curved chalk.
They sit, staring always ahead,
not seeing a world of strangers
edging past them
with only the hint of a smile.

K-Things
I sit in my kitchen
And think of some things:
  Of kites and kimonos,
  Of kittens and kings,
  Of kindness and kisses
While my kettle sings.

—Gene Fehler

66 One afternoon at an arts and crafts exhibition, an artist named Marcie shared a booth with me. As she sketched chalk portraits of passersby, I wrote the following poem. When I finished, I was surprised to see that I had used several examples of alliteration, without consciously trying. Can you find them? Hint: Look for *b's, c's, w's,* and *s's.*

"Another time, I consciously played around with alliteration and came up with a simple list of items in 'K-Things.' **99**

Writing Opportunity

Experiment with alliteration in a poem of your own.

❝ In this poem, I used several onomatopoetic words to try to recreate the sounds made by various sports equipment.

"Children often express surprise (even amazement) when I tell them that a major magazine paid me two hundred dollars for the right to publish 'My Sports Onomatopoeia.' They all understand that they were just as capable of writing the poem. Given the idea for the poem (the sounds made by sports equipment), virtually anyone could come up with appropriate words. Luckily for me, I came up with the idea first! ❞

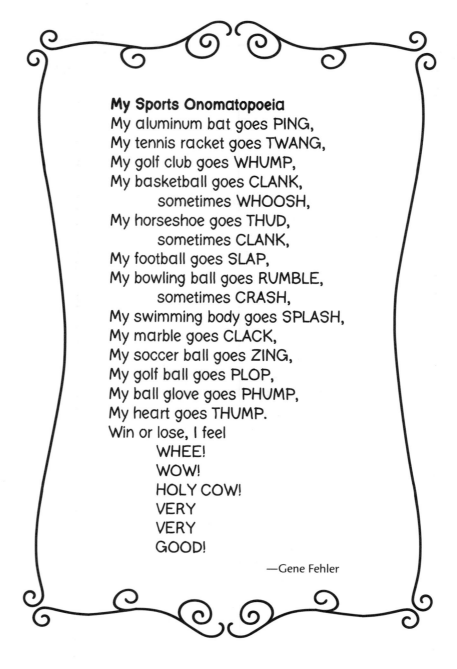

My Sports Onomatopoeia
My aluminum bat goes PING,
My tennis racket goes TWANG,
My golf club goes WHUMP,
My basketball goes CLANK,
            sometimes WHOOSH,
My horseshoe goes THUD,
            sometimes CLANK,
My football goes SLAP,
My bowling ball goes RUMBLE,
            sometimes CRASH,
My swimming body goes SPLASH,
My marble goes CLACK,
My soccer ball goes ZING,
My golf ball goes PLOP,
My ball glove goes PHUMP,
My heart goes THUMP.
Win or lose, I feel
        WHEE!
        WOW!
        HOLY COW!
        VERY
        VERY
        GOOD!

—Gene Fehler

Writing Opportunity

Write a poem in which you use at least two onomatopoetic words. An even greater challenge is to use as many of these words as possible.

CHAPTER FOUR

Rhymes and Fixed Forms

Time for Rhyme

In earlier chapters we looked at a few rhymed poems. We will now take a closer look at some of the fun we can have with rhyme. We'll also examine some of the challenges it presents. Selecting the best possible word for a poem is quite a significant endeavor, whether we're writing fixed form poetry or free verse.

Rhyming Dictionary

No credible craftsperson—carpenter, mechanic, electrician, or maintenance person—would try to execute his or her craft without proper tools. As a writer, you should consider dictionaries, reference works, and entire libraries as essential tools of your craft.

If you're planning to write rhymed poems, find a good rhyming dictionary. For example, you might be able to think of six or seven words that rhyme with *cloak*. But if you use *The Penguin Rhyming Dictionary* (Penguin Books, 1985), you will find at least 52 words that rhyme with *cloak*. Remember that a good dictionary "knows" more words than you do.

Couplets and Quatrains

A *couplet* is two consecutive rhymed lines. Once you can write couplets and have developed a good ear for consistent metrical patterns, you are ready to try writing *quatrains*—four-line stanzas.

What are the benefits and pleasures of writing a complete poem in just four lines?

- You can write a rough draft in a reasonably short time.

- You can create pleasing sounds through the use of rhythm and rhyme.

- You can practice developing your craft with no wasted words or extra syllables.

Poetic Principle

Every poet needs a good rhyming dictionary.

The AABB Quatrain

The simplest form of quatrain is a set of *couplets*. The rhyme scheme is AABB; the first and second lines rhyme, and the third and fourth lines rhyme. Keep in mind that most poems are longer than a single quatrain; longer poems usually use the same rhyme pattern in each quatrain. Look for the couplets in poems such as "By Book or by Crook" (page 88) and "The Balloon" (pages 89 and 90).

The ABCB Quatrain

One of the most common forms of quatrain uses the ABCB rhyme scheme—only the second and fourth lines rhyme. This is one of the easiest forms to write since the third line is not bound by rhyme. With this form, you have some of the freedom of free verse. You also have the greatest opportunity to change your original idea and branch off in a totally different direction. Look for this rhyme scheme in the instructional quatrains on page 70.

Other Quatrains

Another common rhyme scheme is the ABAB quatrain—the first and third lines rhyme, and the second and fourth lines rhyme. With this form, the poet has to be extremely selective in his or her word choice. This process involves a great deal of experimentation. Explore this rhyme scheme in the weather quatrains on page 71.

A less common quatrain form is the ABBA quatrain. The great English poet Alfred "Lord" Tennyson was an acknowledged master of this form.

The Clerihew

The *clerihew* is a fun type of rhymed poem named after its originator, Edmund Clerihew Bentley. This light verse is a quatrain of two couplets. The first line ends with the name of a famous person. The second line, of any length, rhymes with the person's name. The closing couplet generally makes a humorous or "tongue-in-cheek" comment about the person, sometimes using *hyperbole* (exaggeration) to make the point.

A unique feature of these couplets is that they need not follow any precise rhythmic pattern. One line can be long, the next short. There is no set length. Look for the clerihews about famous people on page 72.

Poetic Principle

Rhymed words should always make some kind of sense,
even in a nonsense limerick.

The Sonnet

A *sonnet* consists of 14 ten-syllable lines. The most common form is the English or Shakespearean sonnet, named after William Shakespeare. This sonnet actually consists of four ABAB quatrains and a closing couplet. Thus, its rhyme scheme is ABAB CDCD EFEF GG. This rhyme scheme was used in "Tire Swing" (page 8).

A less common type of sonnet is the Italian or Petrarchan sonnet, named after the Italian writer, Francesco Petrarca. The Italian sonnet consists of an *octave* (eight-line stanza with an ABBAABBA rhyme scheme and a *sestet* (six-line stanza with a rhyme scheme that can be CDCDCD or CDECDE).

Take a few moments to read the sonnets in this book, including "God, Trying to Bring Spring" (page 73) and "On First Looking at a Mantle Homer" (page 74).

Note: A sonnet traditionally uses *iambic pentameter*. An *iamb* is a metrical pattern consisting of two syllables; the second syllable is accented. Five iambs in one line make up a *pentameter line*. (One syllable group, or foot, per line would be *monometer*; two, *dimeter*; three, *trimeter*; four, *tetrameter*; six, *hexameter*; seven, *heptameter*; and eight, *octometer*.)

Four other basic metrical patterns, or feet, are *trochee* (two syllables, the first accented), *anapest* (three syllables, the third accented), *dactyl* (three syllables, the first accented), and *spondee* (one syllable, accented). Take time to examine various metrical patterns if you are going to study poetry or if you plan to write metrical poetry.

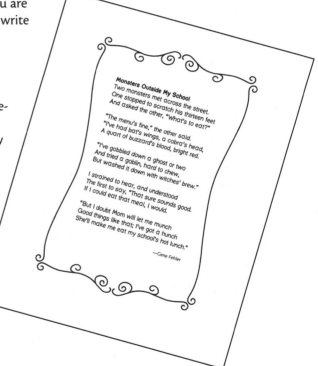

Monsters Outside My School

Two monsters met across the street.
One stopped to scratch his thirteen feet
And asked the other, "What's to eat?"

"The menu's fine," the other said.
"I've had bat's wings, a cobra's head,
A quart of buzzard's blood, bright red.

"I've gobbled down a ghost or two
And tried a goblin, hard to chew,
But washed it down with witches' brew."

I strained to hear, and understood
The first to say, "That sure sounds good.
If I could eat that meal, I would.

"But I doubt Mom will let me munch
Good things like that; I've got a hunch
She'll make me eat my school's hot lunch."

—Gene Fehler

The Tercet

A *tercet* uses single rhymes and three-line stanzas. If all three lines rhyme consecutively, the stanza is traditionally called a *triplet*. If the lines rhyme alternately—the second line rhyming with the first line of the next stanza—the form is known as *terza rima*. Share "Monsters Outside My School" (page 75) with a friend.

Poetic Principle

You have to have a reason to rhyme.
Rhymed words have to fit the sense of your poem.

Other Rhyme Patterns

Rhyme is still possible in free verse poems such as "Jungle Warfare" (page 32). *Random rhyme* means that two or more of the lines may rhyme. Poets use this rhyme form to improve the flow, fun, or meaning of their poems.

In most poems, however, the story, idea, or experience is the key; the rhyme is merely incidental. So, sometimes it's fun to experiment with rhyme sounds and to try to write a poem that has its origin in rhyme. Look for the single rhyme pattern in "Worms Are Good" (page 76).

If you enjoy playing with rhyme, you might try some of the many other more complex rhymed patterns, such as the *rondeau, rondel, villanelle, triolet,* and *sestina.* If you are ready to experiment with them, then go to a library or bookstore and find a book that provides an in-depth look at various rhyming forms.

 How Do I Find Rhyming Lines?

Often the choices of rhyme you are left with for your second, third, or fourth line won't work. You seem unable to come up with a thought that fits the sense of your poem. When that happens, too many aspiring poets fall into the trap of using one of those rhymes anyway and destroying the coherence of their poems. They are left with a rhyme, but often this is not enough to carry the poem, to make it meaningful, or to make it of lasting interest to the reader.

 Writing Opportunity

Here are the first three lines of a quatrain. See if you can write a suitable fourth line for it. Try to match the rhyme and rhythm of line three.

A Child's First Drawings

They're mysteries to grown-up's eyes,
Those horses, houses in disguise;
My child thinks I'm not too smart

—Gene Fehler

Compare your fourth line with the following.

Author's fourth line:

'Cause I can't tell the two apart.

Selecting the best possible word for a poem is a challenge,
whether you're writing fixed form poetry or free verse.

What can you do if you can't find a rhyming word that works?

- Change the first line to give yourself a different end word to rhyme with.

- Change the entire format of your poem. Perhaps your idea will work better in free verse form.

- Completely change the story or idea of your poem. Perhaps a rhyming word will lead you in a totally different direction from your preconceived notion.

And Now for Some Poems

The remainder of this chapter presents poems on assorted topics that demonstrate various rhymes and fixed forms of poetry, including *quatrains, sonnets, clerihews, tercets,* and *single rhyme verse.* These pages also include challenging opportunities for you to experiment with writing your own rhymed and fixed form poetry.

Poetic Principle

A poem will often suggest more questions than answers.

Keep Your Eyes on the Ball
Keep your eyes on the ball
And your bat off your shoulder,
And you'll be a hitter
Before you're much older.

Where to Run When You Hit the Ball
Of all base-running blunders
Perhaps the very worst
Is when a batter hits the ball
Then runs toward third, not first.

Pitching a Spitball
To pitch a spitball is an act
You're likely to regret,
Especially if it's juicy
And gets everybody wet.

You and the Umpire
Jaw with the umpire;
Call him a name.
That's how to get yourself
Tossed from the game.

—Gene Fehler

Writing Opportunity

Choose a topic of personal interest to you. Write a series of three or four quatrains using the flexible ABCB rhyme scheme. See if it will open the door to a wide range of approaches to your topic.

Cloudburst

A cloudburst is more picturesque
    Than is a quiet sprinkle.
I sit entranced behind my desk
    And watch the windows wrinkle.

Dew

It sparkles on the tint of grass
    At break of day on green of lawn.
For beauty, little can surpass
    That loveliest of times—the dawn.

Frost

It looks like snow, but isn't quite,
    That thin, white layer of April chill.
It creeps toward blossoms in the night
    And cripples with unlikely skill.

Ice Storms

The crinkle, crackle of the ice
    And glitter, gleaming of the sun
Create an artist's paradise.
    But limbs of trees don't have much fun.

Thunder

Volcano, earthquake, forest fire
    Make a trio, quite subdued
When we compare it to a choir
    Of the thunder's magnitude.

—Gene Fehler

❝ I used the ABAB rhyme scheme to write a series of quatrains about various forms of weather. **❞**

Writing Opportunity

Using the ABAB rhyme scheme, write a quatrain about any topic. It might be fun to experiment with the quatrains you wrote in some other form (AABB or ABCB) and see how your ideas change because of the new restrictions.

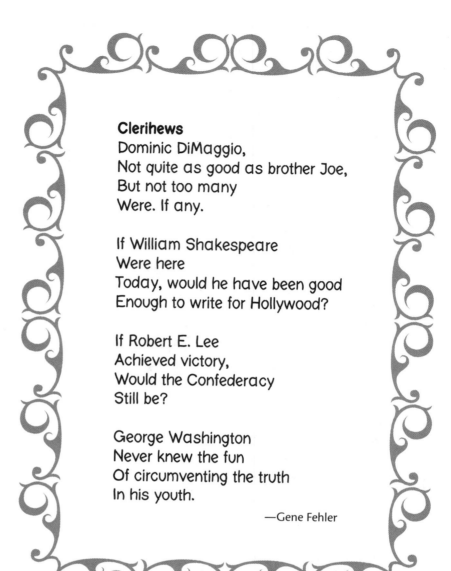

Clerihews

Dominic DiMaggio,
Not quite as good as brother Joe,
But not too many
Were. If any.

If William Shakespeare
Were here
Today, would he have been good
Enough to write for Hollywood?

If Robert E. Lee
Achieved victory,
Would the Confederacy
Still be?

George Washington
Never knew the fun
Of circumventing the truth
In his youth.

—Gene Fehler

Writing Opportunity

Make a list of 20 famous people from walks of life such as sports, entertainment, science, politics, history, and literature. Try to write clerihews about as many of these people as possible.

God, Promising to End Winter

I think that spring's afraid to budge
From winter's grasping misery.
I'll bend to give it one small nudge,
Enough to send it spinning free.

I know the joys my nudge will bring:
Warm breezes, green grass, baseball games,
The laugh of children, birds that sing
In praise of all that spring reclaims.

Yet winter still maintains its grip:
It clings like fresh-taped bloody gauze.
Since nudging did not work, I'll rip
The tape to earn the town's applause.

God, Trying to Bring Spring

God notices that spring's afraid to budge
From nasty winter's grasping misery.
So He decides to give it one small nudge,
A tiny one to send it spinning free.
He knows the joys His little nudge will bring:
Warm breezes, green grass, flowers, baseball games,
The laughs of children, chirping birds that sing
In praise of all the pleasures spring reclaims.
Yet winter still maintains its painful grip:
It clings like sticky fresh-taped bloody gauze.
Since nudging did not work, now God must rip
The winter's tape to earn the world's applause.
　　Of all God's tasks, by far the hardest thing
　　Is turning stubborn winter into spring.

—Gene Fehler

> 66 I wrote a poem about how anxious I was for spring to come. Later, I decided to rewrite it as an English sonnet. Notice that what was originally a 12-line poem needed to be 14 lines. Also, I had to give each line ten syllables instead of eight. 99

Writing Opportunity

Try writing your own sonnet. One way to begin is to take one of your earlier quatrains and consider ways to expand it into a longer poem. Pay close attention to the rhyme scheme and metrical pattern.

On First Looking at a Mantle Homer

Long had I had the pleasure to behold
The New York Yankees on the TV screen.
They played just like a powerful machine
And much good baseball drama did unfold.
Oft of Mantle's power I had been told,
But not a single homerun had I seen
Which cleared the wall in Mantle's own demesne:
Death Valley, where homeruns were rare as gold.
And then one day 'neath summer's sunlit skies
The Mick stepped to the plate with boyish grin
And swung; a hard line drive began to rise
Far over heads of unbelieving men,
So far that even now I realize
That I will not see Mantle's like again.

—Gene Fehler

Writing Opportunity

Write a poem of any length or form (rhymed or free verse) about one of your favorite people. The person can be real or fictitious, living or dead, famous or familiar.

Monsters Outside My School
Two monsters met across the street.
One stopped to scratch his thirteen feet
And asked the other, "What's to eat?"

"The menu's fine," the other said.
"I've had bat's wings, a cobra's head,
A quart of buzzard's blood, bright red.

"I've gobbled down a ghost or two
And tried a goblin, hard to chew,
But washed it down with witches' brew."

I strained to hear, and understood
The first to say, "That sure sounds good.
If I could eat that meal, I would.

"But I doubt Mom will let me munch
Good things like that; I've got a hunch
She'll make me eat my school's hot lunch."
—Gene Fehler

A Word from the Poet

❝ I have nothing but respect for the thousands of dedicated school cafeteria workers around the country who try their best to provide children with delicious, nutritious hot lunches. However, I have occasionally come across students who feel sorry for the monster who had to eat cafeteria fare in this tercet. **❞**

Writing Opportunity

Try to tell a story in tercets, using the same rhyme sound in all three lines of each stanza.

A Word from the Poet

66 No specific event inspired this poem. It was merely an experiment in rhyme, and you will notice that the same rhyme sound is repeated in each of the ten lines.

"But after writing the poem, I recalled an event that took place when I was eight years old and playing with my friend in his yard. I bit into an apple, chewed, and swallowed. Then I saw half a worm wriggling in the part of the apple that remained.

"Worms are good. Sure they are. **99**

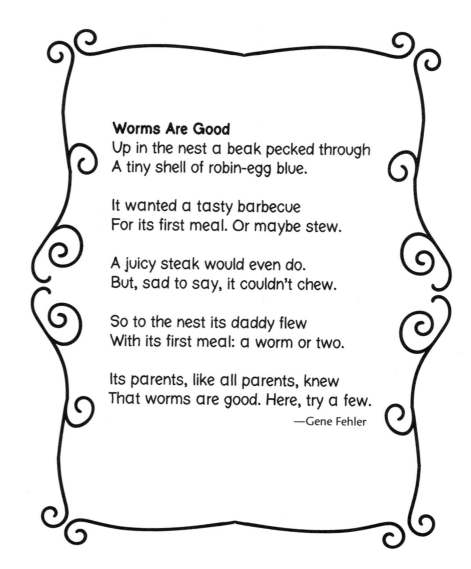

Worms Are Good
Up in the nest a beak pecked through
A tiny shell of robin-egg blue.

It wanted a tasty barbecue
For its first meal. Or maybe stew.

A juicy steak would even do.
But, sad to say, it couldn't chew.

So to the nest its daddy flew
With its first meal: a worm or two.

Its parents, like all parents, knew
That worms are good. Here, try a few.

—Gene Fehler

Writing Opportunity

Choose one particular rhyming sound—use a rhyming dictionary if you wish. Write down as many words as you can think of with that sound. Then try to write a poem using that same rhyming sound at the end of each line. Make the poem as long as you wish, but work hard on the sense of the poem as well as the sound.

CHAPTER FIVE

Making Revisions

◎ R-E-V-I-S-I-O-N

Unrevised writing is like food without seasoning or a doctor without medicine—simply not as good as it could be. Since all writing is a matter of choices, poems (free verse and fixed form) go through countless drafts in which the poet experiments with ideas and language, structure and form. Sometimes *how* you say something can contribute as much to your poem's success as *what* you say. That is where revision comes in.

◎ Drafting a Poem

Many writers feel that their poems are never good enough. There is almost always more that can be done in the revision process. Only after having re-routed countless drafts to the wastebasket and going to the dictionary a hundred times can they finally move on to another poem.

Writing rhymed poems presents additional challenges as poets seek to master and polish the rhymes and make their meters as consistent as possible. Read the accounts of the steps I took to revise my drafts of several poems, including "Seventh Round" (pages 81 and 82), "Bone Burying" (pages 83 and 84), "The Longest Hit" (pages 85 and 86), and "By Book or by Crook" (pages 87 and 88). These honest accounts will help you realize that poets exert much patience and careful scrutiny to produce their best efforts.

◎ How Should My Poem "Look"?

There is no firm set of rules to follow when determining a poem's form. Nevertheless, unrhymed poems often have lines with fewer than four or five words; and the lines should not go all the way to the right-hand margin.

Poets use their intuition to decide what looks right on the page and what sounds best when read aloud. They often retype their poems in many different forms until they find the one that works best for them. I chose to write "My Pitching Lullaby" and "The Snow and the Heat" (pages 61 and 62) as long, skinny poems with only one or two words on most of the lines, because they looked good that way. Our sense of form is influenced by the poets we read; and the more we read, the wider our range of options. Consider the original shape of the poem about baseball pitcher Camilo Pascual (page 91).

Poetic Principle

No matter how good a poet you think you are,
you're never quite as good as you can be.

What About Capitalization?

The use of capitalization in poetry is essentially a matter of personal choice. In the past, the first word on each line was almost always capitalized; today, it is often not, especially in free verse poems. Again, the poet often bases his or her decision on what looks best on the page. Here are two suggestions:

- Capitalize the first word of each line in most rhymed poems.

- Do not capitalize the first word of each line in most free verse poems, especially if the lines are short.

Hints for Revising Poems

Use these practical tips when you revise your poems:

- Carefully read the words and thoughts you have written.

- When you want to tell the reader something, try to figure out how you can show it. What other details can you add?

- Choose the best possible words. There's always more than one way to say something. Sometimes your second choice will be better than your first.

- Don't always write in complete sentences. Leave out unnecessary words.

- Avoid using a person's real name, and NEVER use the real name if it would prove embarrassing or might make someone feel bad.

- Write your poem like a poem. Try different forms and choose the one that looks best.

- You have to have a reason to rhyme. Your rhymed word has to fit the sense of your poem.

- Deciding when to end a poem is always a challenge. Less is often better.

- Choose your title carefully. Experiment with several ideas.

- Copy your poem neatly on the page. Make sure you use correct spelling and grammar.

Poetic Principle

Don't stay with your original idea if you get a better one.

Titles ARE Important

A title is an integral part of the poem and helps communicate your mood or idea to the reader. A good title can help sell your poem to a publisher; a poorly chosen title can help get your poem rejected. Sometimes poets simply use the first line as the poem's title, and occasionally they call their poems "Untitled." Avoid using abstract titles such as "Love," "Hate," "Death," or "Nature." Many editors consider an abstract title to be a crucial strike against you before they even reach your first line. While sometimes a poem is good enough to overcome an abstract title, why take the risk?

Read how important titles are in "My Lost Classmate" (page 92) and "Where to See Strength" (page 93).

Listening to Others

Sometimes we write a brilliant poem that no one appreciates. But more often we write a good poem that could become brilliant, or at least better, if we were willing to listen to other people's opinions. Readers can often help us see what's not working in a poem. Perhaps we've used the second best word instead of the best one, or we're a little off in our rhythm. We might be telling too much instead of showing, or perhaps we can give our poem a sharper focus.

If you want to write poetry, you must be willing to recognize that your poem always retains the potential for change, often change for the better. It really doesn't matter how well a line works for the poet if it doesn't work for at least some readers. However, you won't know until you try.

Publishing Is Not the "End-All"

Many poets are in a BIG hurry to have their words printed in a book, newspaper, or magazine. Once a poem is accepted for publication, some poets cease to work on that piece of writing. But satisfaction doesn't come from publication; it comes from knowing that each line and each word is the best you could come up with. Even after a poem has been accepted by a publisher and appeared in print, we should still try to make it the best poem we can.

Examine the histories of poems that have continued to change after their publication (pages 87–90). These pieces demonstrate that publishing is NOT the end-all for a poem.

And Now for Some Poems

The poems in this chapter provide specific examples of ways in which I revised words, rhymes, meter, and titles in my poems. Most poems also include opportunities for you to revise and improve the quality of your own writing.

Poetic Principle

Other people can often help you see what's not
working in a poem.

A Word from the Poet

❝ I once wrote what I thought would be a very short poem titled 'Thoughts During the Eighteenth Mile of My First Marathon.' I was not writing from experience. The farthest I'd ever run nonstop was nine miles, and a marathon is slightly over 26. But judging from how I felt after those nine miles, I tried to imagine the feelings of someone running over twice that distance.

"My poem went like this:
*The one thing I can't do
During that awful
   eighteenth mile . . .
   is smile.*

"I showed the poem to a group of writing friends, but no one liked it. So I decided to try again. This time I added more details to show what was going on during the run. After a few revisions, my three-line poem turned into one with 17 lines. ❞

Thoughts During the Eighteenth Mile of My First Marathon

Uphill toward the burning sun
I run. You call this fun?

I falter, try to keep my pace,
stay in the race
by tossing water in my face.

I start to feel
the growing blister on my heel,
the throbbing pain inside my brain.
My muscles strain.

Blurs of runners thunder past me
as my legs begin to slow.
Eight miles to go.
Can I finish? I don't know.

All the while I run this mile
(this awful awful eighteenth mile)
the one thing I can't do
   is smile.

—Gene Fehler

Writing Opportunity

Think of some of the times when the reality of an experience differed from your expectations. Write about it.

Seventh Round (early draft)
The fighter's left jab
is like a piston
driving against his
opponent's head.
It snaps the head back
and sets him up
for a flurry of punches.
Finally he throws
a hard right that breaks
his opponent's nose
and sends him, bloodied,
to the canvas.
The bell sounds,
ending the round.

—Gene Fehler

A Word from the Poet

66 I'm not a fan of boxing, but I have written a poem or two about the sport. When I have the idea for a poem, I often use prose to quickly write some of what I hope to say. My first attempt at 'Seventh Round' appears here.

"I played around with the form to see if I could make it look like a poem. This was a beginning, but my poem was basically prose broken up into short lines. It did too much telling. I needed to look at the boxing match and show the reader exactly what I saw happening in the ring. So I began to get rid of unnecessary "telling" words. I didn't want to tell about the left jab, I wanted to *show* it: *the left jab, like a piston driving the head back.* **99**

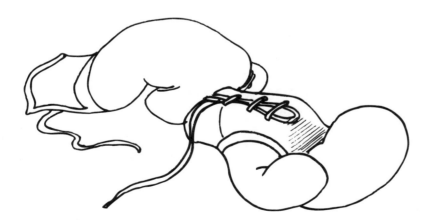

❝ I went through my draft, line by line, changing from telling to showing. With each new draft I experimented with form, trying to find the best possible way to break the lines. I finally ended up with a form that I thought seemed to work best for this particular poem. Through repetition I was trying not only to show the reader how the punches *looked,* but also how they *felt.* And although I didn't make any explicit statement in the poem about what I think of boxing, my words and style presented an implicit expression of my feelings.

"Maybe 'Seventh Round' would be even more powerful if I wrote in first person instead of third. Maybe I should be the winning boxer, maybe I should be the losing one. These are some of the great joys of writing poems—the endless questions, the countless options, the weighing of alternatives.

"Here is the completed version of 'Seventh Round.' ❞

Seventh Round (final draft)
the left jab, like a piston
driving,

driving against the head
snapping,

snapping the head back,
setting

him up for the flurry of
punches:

right, left, right, left, right,
left

and then the hard right that
spins

him face down on canvas
bloodied

beneath the broken nose
twisted;

and the bell clangs,
saving

him for yet another
round

—Gene Fehler

Writing Opportunity

Take a look at some of the poems you have written, and choose one of your favorites. Read it carefully and find a word or a line that you can change. You might be surprised to find that your poems can change.

Bone Burying (early draft)

*"If a dog digs a big hole in your garden
there will be a death in the family."*
—Gypsy belief

Deep.
Deeper.
Fudgie digs
until the bone
large as Christmas
rests
under a scattering
of dirt,
a future feast
hidden from
neighborhood hounds.

My sons and I
laugh
at her half-blind
search
for spies.
Her secret is safe:
we do not care about
Gypsy beliefs,
read our horoscopes,
or fear
black cats.

—Gene Fehler

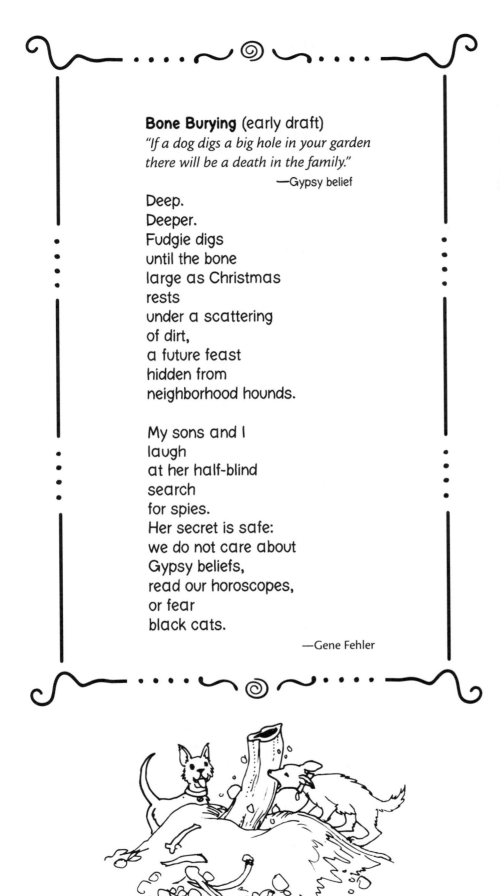

66 I submitted the poem on page 83 to *Sun Dog* and received this note from its editor: *I think I would rewrite that second stanza. The first stanza, title, and quote are so appealing. Keep at it.*

"I sort of liked my second stanza, but I remembered that the success of a poem depends on how much emotion the reader feels when reading it—not on how much you feel as a poet. So I played around with the poem for a long time and totally changed its focus and tone.

"This is how my final draft was published in *Sun Dog.* 99

Bone Burying (final draft)
"If a dog digs a big hole in your garden there will be a death in the family."
—Gypsy belief

Deep.
Deeper.
The dog next door digs
until the bone
large as Christmas
rests
under a scattering
of dirt,
a future feast
hidden from
neighborhood hounds.

I pause from my hedge-
trimming,
wait in vain
for the familiar
screendoor slamming,
for the broom-wielding
lady of the house
rushing
to save her tomatoes.
She is out shopping,
perhaps,
or taking an afternoon nap.

—Gene Fehler

Writing
Opportunity

Take one of your poems and copy the first stanza just as it is. Then change the second stanza. Disregard the thought of your original poem. You might end up going in a completely new direction.

Once you have finished your new second stanza, go back and make all the necessary changes to your first. If you have additional stanzas, change them as needed.

The Longest Hit (early draft)
The longest hit I've ever seen
Was made last night by Billy
Green.

He hit a fast ball with such power
It sailed above our water tower.

It traveled so far through the night
It barely missed a satellite.

I believe the baseball hit the moon!
Gee, I hope it comes down soon.

—Gene Fehler

66 One of the traps I fall into is thinking that readers will read my poems the same way I do. I have a hard time realizing that the poems themselves must establish the rhythm; the reader isn't going to hear the poet's actual voice reading it aloud.

"In 'The Longest Hit,' I read line five like this: *It traveled so far through the night*. However, an editor pointed out that the natural rhythm would make most people read it like this: *It traveled so far through the night*. This wouldn't be consistent with the iambic pattern I had established earlier.

"The editor also said that there was a problem in the seventh line. The two-syllable word *believe* threw off the basic rhythmic pattern. Without realizing it, I was inconsistent in the rhythmic pattern throughout my poem. As a result, readers might find the poem awkward and amateurish.

"Here is how the poem first looked. 99

❝ I made these changes in the last four lines—not changing the meaning, but trying to smooth out the rhythm. And I think the poem is better now. However, the final line is only seven syllables, and begins with an accented syllable. The line works for me, but I'm going to ask for feedback from other poets and readers whose opinions I respect to try to determine whether that last line needs to be changed.

"Here is 'The Longest Hit' as it now looks. **❞**

The Longest Hit (final draft)
The longest hit I've ever seen
Was made last night by Billy Green.

He hit a fast ball with such power
It sailed above our water tower.

It traveled far into the night
And barely missed a satellite.

The baseball bounced right off the moon!
Gee, I hope it comes down soon.

—Gene Fehler

Writing Opportunity

Experiment with couplets. Write a simple line of eight syllables (da-DA da-DA da-DA da-DA). Then write a second line with the same pattern and with an end word that rhymes with the one in the first. Try to develop a feel for consistent rhythm and select rhymed words that best advance the thought of the first line.

A Word from the Poet

Reader Involvement (first draft)
One night at dark I took a look
Inside a neat detective book
And saw a prowler crouched inside.
He couldn't hide, although he tried,
So then he spun, pulled out a gun,
Shot wildly and began to run.
I turned the pages, kept in sight
The prowler in his frantic flight.
I wasn't scared, I read it all,
And saw the prowler trip and fall.
The policemen caught him, he was jailed.
I'm glad to say that right prevailed.
That prowler now is doing time
In prison somewhere for his crime.
I like to believe I had a say
In helping put that thief away,
So I will keep on reading books
And aid in capturing those crooks.

—Gene Fehler

66 I had an idea for a poem about a child reading a detective book and really 'getting into' the story. I didn't know how the poem was going to end, but I let one rhyme lead into another until I ended up with a complete story. My finished poem, which I submitted to *Pennywhistle Press*, looked like this. (See 'Reader Involvement' at left.)

"The editor wrote back with the good news that he would publish my poem. However, he asked if he could change my title—he didn't much care for it. I didn't have any strong emotional attachment to the title 'Reader Involvement' and willingly gave it up.

"Then I took a closer look at the rest of the poem. The first line jumped out at me and made me cringe: *One night at dark. . . .* Does one really need to qualify night as dark? What are the alternatives? I wrote to the editor and requested that they change the first line. I gave them about three acceptable alternatives and they chose *One quiet night. . . .* 99

❝ After the poem was published, I was overjoyed to see it in print. It was displayed with full-color illustrations and a much better title than my somewhat dreary 'Reader Involvement.'

"But then I was dismayed to see two other lines that should have been better. In the second line, the word *neat* bothered me. *Neat* is a word a child might use, but was it the best word? I decided to change it to *tense*. The last line *And aid in capturing those crooks* also seemed weak, so I substituted *And help to capture all those crooks* in case the poem was later printed elsewhere.

"The present version of the poem—but possibly not the ultimate one—reads like this. **❞**

By Book or by Crook (final draft)
One quiet night I took a look
Inside a tense detective book
And saw a prowler crouched inside.
He couldn't hide, although he tried,
So then he spun, pulled out a gun,
Shot wildly and began to run.
I turned the pages, kept in sight
The prowler in his frantic flight.
I wasn't scared, I read it all,
And saw the prowler trip and fall.
The policemen caught him, he was jailed.
I'm glad to say that right prevailed.
That prowler now is doing time
In prison somewhere for his crime.
I like to believe I had a say
In helping put that thief away,
So I will keep on reading books
And help to capture all those crooks.

—Gene Fehler

Writing Opportunity

Use rhymed couplets to tell a short story.

The Balloon

When he was eight and feeling sad,
He blew all of the love he had
Into a balloon of gleaming blue.
And as he did, the small boy knew

That when the sides were stretched out wide
And all the love was packed inside,
The balloon would be a balloon no more
but some close friend he'd waited for

Who wouldn't fight him, yell or scream,
Or wake him trembling from a dream.
He held the balloon against his face;
It seemed as soft as an embrace.

His eyes were closed and didn't see
His older sister, Emily,
With glinting eyes and hateful grin
Come sneaking near him with a pin.

continued…

—Gene Fehler

66 Of all my poems, my wife Polly's all-time favorite is 'The Balloon.' This is a story poem written in rhymed couplets about a small boy his balloon, and an older sister. Perhaps Polly admires its narrative, rather than poetic, aspect. It is certainly sentimental, and I know poets who frown on sentimentality. But to me, if a poem stirs the emotions, it is successful.

"By the way, after this poem was published I was embarrassed to show people the printed version. Why? Because I hated the last line of stanza four (*Come burst his balloon with just a pin*). I changed that offending line to *Come sneaking near him with a pin*. It's funny how much better you can feel about your poem and your-self just by changing a word or two. **99**

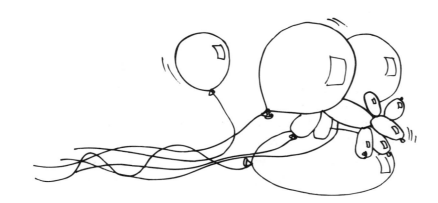

The Balloon, continued...

The balloon exploded in his ear.
He jumped back startled, filled with fear.
He heard her laughing at her joke;
He watched her laugh, and then he spoke:

"I know you tried to make me cry,
But look, you see, my eyes are dry.
Your pin just broke the outside skin,
It couldn't break what I put in.

"That balloon was filled with more than air,
A lot of love was packed in there;
And when it burst, that love all flew.
I'll bet some even flew on you."

She shook her head. It was absurd
To think he'd said what she had heard.
She tried to laugh at what he'd said.
She tried, but smiled, with love, instead.

—Gene Fehler

Writing Opportunity

Often one of the first objects of our affection is an inanimate object like the balloon. Did you ever have a teddy bear, doll, or stuffed animal of which you were (or perhaps still are) quite fond? If so, share some details so your readers might see and understand the basis for your affection.

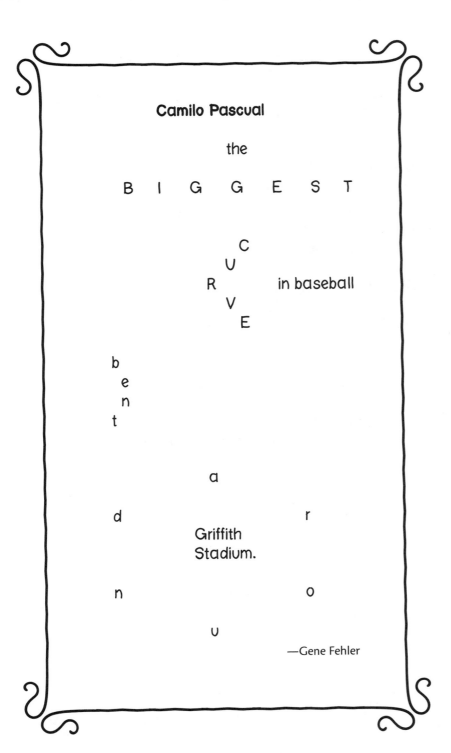

Camilo Pascual

the

B I G G E S T

C
U
R   in baseball
V
E

b
e
n
t

a

d   r

Griffith
Stadium.

n   o

u

—Gene Fehler

A Word from the Poet

❝ Look at this 'poem' about former big league baseball pitcher Camilo Pascual.

"I played around with the form of this poem. Here's my final version. Through the arrangement of my words you will see that I tried to 'show' that Pascual threw an excellent curve ball. ❞

Writing Opportunity

Experiment with form and typography. Write a poem about any subject in which an unusual arrangement of words on the page is one of its key features. You may want to arrange the words in the shape of the thing you're writing the poem about.

❝ A fourth-grade class asked me to write this narrative about a classmate who had moved away. When I read the poem to the class, they thought a better title would be 'Her Final Kiss.' I think they may be right. ❞

My Lost Classmate

My classmate moved away last year.
    My life is sad without her here.
I can't forget that awful day
    She said she had to move away.

She told me she would keep in touch.
    "You know I'll miss you very much."
That's what she said. She said, "I'll write."
    She took my hand and held it tight.

She leaned to me and kissed my cheek.
    My knees went weak; I couldn't speak.
A teardrop glistened in her eyes
    When we'd completed our good-byes.

She said she'd send me her address,
    But where she is, I cannot guess.
For months I watched for that first note.
    I wonder if she ever wrote.

Time separates us now, and space.
    My hand moves gently to my face.
I touch my cheek and feel still
    Her final kiss, and always will.

—Gene Fehler

Where to See Strength

The lightning chain, the tree and rock,
    The face that's given up its hate.
The grace from pain, the steel lock
    That clanks across the prison's gate.

The mountain's peak, the bars of steel,
    The burst of rushing waterfall.
The classic Greek, the churchbell's peal,
    The ringing of the patriot's call.

The muscles taut, the burst of sun,
    The mother with her newborn foal.
The storm's onslaught, the fight begun,
    The suffering of the human soul.

—Gene Fehler

66 I constructed this poem from a list of things that have strength. Yet the word *strength* never appears in the body of the poem. Without the title, the reader might not see what the items in the list have in common. **99**

Writing Opportunity

Go back over all the poems you have written and make sure each one is titled. Now look carefully at each title. Can you make it less abstract? Can you come up with titles that are interesting, yet not misleading? Can you come up with titles that help communicate the idea or tone of the poem without revealing too much?

imitation and inspiration

From Reading to Writing

We have focused on using our experiences, observations, and imaginations as sources of ideas for poems. But what about using ideas that come from reading other people's writing? With the millions of books and poems that have already been written, little remains that is completely original. In fact, many of the great works of literature have been suggested by earlier writings.

As we read, we often come across an idea, setting, character, or plot that intrigues us. Something might strike us as so interesting, emotional, or memorable that we are moved to write about it. Or we might take a phrase, word, or idea from a single line in someone else's poem and then branch off in a totally new direction.

Imitation or Inspiration?

We obviously need to guard against plagiarizing—stealing someone else's language. But no one thinks or writes in a vacuum. Most ideas, settings, characters, and plots have already been used in some form. Our job is not necessarily to begin with something that is totally new and untouched by previous writers; rather, it is to find a new shape, approach, or vision.

Most poets have written about love. If you were to write a poem about love, perhaps your first kiss, you would not be writing about a new experience. What would be new is your vision or stylistic approach to a common subject. Only by reading widely can you have any sense of whether or not your approach is truly unique.

Using Your Imagination

Most people are amazed to discover the virtually unlimited number of poems that come directly out of personal experience, observation, or reading. And often these episodes can be described exactly as they occurred, without changing a single thing. The only creative aspect is that of finding the best way to shape the detail of the experience into a poem.

On the other hand, while the idea for a poem might be generated by some personal experience or observation, you might invent and change details to make the poem work the way you think it should. Your poem might end up being one percent truth and 99 percent lies!

Poetic Principle

To be a great writer, you must be a great reader!

What About the Narrator?

As you write your poem, you must assume the identity of the narrator. In fact, you can become a new persona in your poems. Your work is not to judge or interpret the poem for your readers. Your job is to share the narrator's experience or observation.

As you explore the poems in this book, look for the narrator's voice. In "An Evening of Roach Killing" (page 26), the narrators are my own sons, and I speak with their voices; in "Late Afternoons" (page 117), a lonely, older woman tells the story; and in "Rats" (page 59), the narrator does something so unexpected that he even surprises me!

Sometimes you may agree with the narrator, and at other times you might not. In "The Day Bennie Missed the Bus" (page 16), you may feel the narrator was a mean person, or you may think the narrator made a wise decision. However, I do not provide my opinion about the narrator's behavior and let readers form their own judgments.

 ## And Now for Some Poems

This chapter is dedicated to exploring ideas for poems inspired by a variety of sources. I used inspiration from poems, books, and movies to write the first series of poems (pages 97–102). These titles include "Watching for Saws," "Cal Norris," and "Sitting by the Phone."

The next group of poems (pages 103–108) came about as a result of something I heard someone say or a topic that someone asked me to write about. These poems include "Slant-In," "My Foolish Friends," and "Skating with Sherri."

The final series of poems (pages 109–117) developed as reflections and products of my own imagination and life experiences. These poems include "My Worst Baseball Experience," "Pet-Owner," and "Deathbed Showdown."

Enjoy using these poems as models to explore assorted themes, forms, and stories. And be sure to add your own measure of imagination to make your writing unique.

Poetic Principle

The poet's job is not to judge, or interpret;
the poet's job is merely to share an experience.

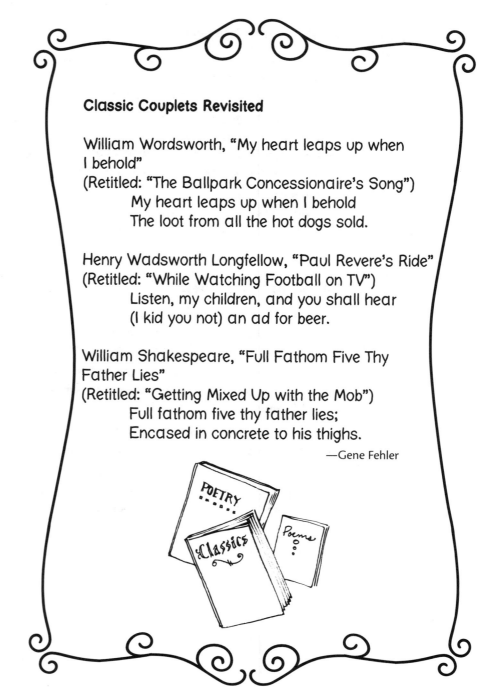

A Word from the Poet

66 A fun way to practice rhymed poetry is to imitate the rhyme patterns you find in other poems. On the simplest level, you can take single lines from famous poems and imitate the rhythm and rhyme of those lines, as I did in some poems I call 'Classic Couplets Revisited.'

"The first line of each couplet is taken directly from a famous poem. I wrote the second line and the new title. But remember, any time you directly quote someone else's work, you must give that person credit. Plagiarism is a serious offense. 99

Classic Couplets Revisited

William Wordsworth, "My heart leaps up when I behold"
(Retitled: "The Ballpark Concessionaire's Song")
    My heart leaps up when I behold
    The loot from all the hot dogs sold.

Henry Wadsworth Longfellow, "Paul Revere's Ride"
(Retitled: "While Watching Football on TV")
    Listen, my children, and you shall hear
    (I kid you not) an ad for beer.

William Shakespeare, "Full Fathom Five Thy Father Lies"
(Retitled: "Getting Mixed Up with the Mob")
    Full fathom five thy father lies;
    Encased in concrete to his thighs.

—Gene Fehler

Writing Opportunity

Select any rhymed poem written by someone else and imitate its rhyme scheme as precisely as possible. Choose a poem that has an unusual rhyme scheme, one that you've seldom seen. You can write your poem about any topic.

Now write a second version of your poem. Try to write it from a different viewpoint, perhaps from that of another participant or an outside observer.

Watching for Saws (early draft)
The saw slipped
on the branch I was trimming
and ground its way
into my thumb.
A fountain of red washed
over my clenched fist.

Later, after the cleansing,
the stitching, the bandages,
I remembered Robert Frost
and the boy who saw all spoiled.
"Don't let him cut my hand off,
the doctor, when he comes."
I thought about how precious
life is, and how fragile,
one moment whistling a melody,
the next trying to keep
the body intact, the blood
from spilling, pain from building.

Later, I did what the boy
in the Frost poem could not do—
returned to complete my task,
my thumb still intact, my life
still a melody, my eyes open
wider to the threat of saws.

—Gene Fehler

A Word from the Poet

66 Sometimes things happen that remind us of something we've read. Once, to make my lawn-mowing task easier, I decided to remove some thin, low-hanging branches. My saw slipped and cut into the end of my thumb. I went inside to stop the bleeding and to wash and bandage the cut. It was not serious, yet I couldn't help but think of one of my favorite poems: 'Out, Out—' by Robert Frost, in which a small boy accidentally saws off his hand and dies.

"When I showed this poem to another writer, she questioned my form. She thought it would be stronger without the enjambment or run-on lines. So I decided to retype 'Watching for Saws' without the run-on lines, and I changed a few words. The poem seemed to fall naturally into four three-line stanzas. You can decide which form works better. 99

Watching for Saws (final draft)
The saw slipped on the branch I was trimming
and ground its way into my thumb.
A fountain of red washed over my clenched hand.

Later, after the cleansing, the stitching, the bandages,
I remembered Robert Frost and the boy who saw all spoiled.
"Don't let him cut my hand off, the doctor, when he comes."

I thought of roads chosen, of roads that choose us,
of one moment whistling a melody, the next trying to keep
the body intact, the blood from spilling, pain from building.

Later, I did what the boy in the Frost poem could not do—
returned to complete my task, my thumb still intact, my life
still a melody, my eyes open wider to the threat of saws.

—Gene Fehler

Writing
Opportunity

Select one of your free verse poems and
rewrite it in several different forms,
without necessarily changing any words.
Use various line lengths, and try breaking
the poem into stanzas of different
lengths. This will help you avoid the trap
of using the same form (often not the
most satisfying one) for every poem.

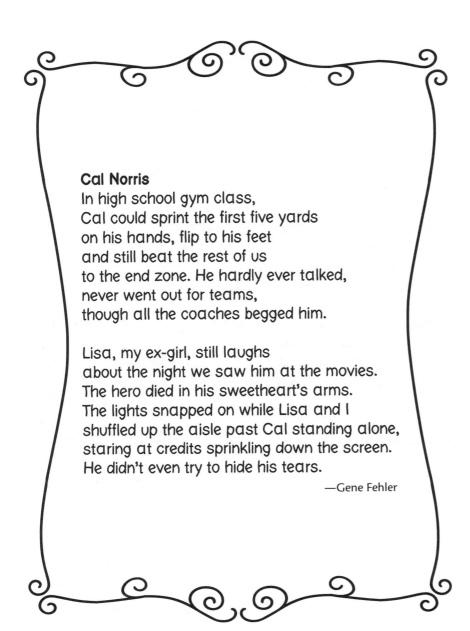

Cal Norris
In high school gym class,
Cal could sprint the first five yards
on his hands, flip to his feet
and still beat the rest of us
to the end zone. He hardly ever talked,
never went out for teams,
though all the coaches begged him.

Lisa, my ex-girl, still laughs
about the night we saw him at the movies.
The hero died in his sweetheart's arms.
The lights snapped on while Lisa and I
shuffled up the aisle past Cal standing alone,
staring at credits sprinkling down the screen.
He didn't even try to hide his tears.

—Gene Fehler

A Word from the Poet

66 I read a poem by Ed Orr titled 'Ralph Ennis.' In his poem, Orr gave a brief character sketch of Ralph (eight short free verse lines).

"I decided to try a character sketch of my own. I wanted to pick someone who 'stood out' and displayed unusual characteristics. I chose Cal Norris, who possesses special athletic skills but is not a 'typical' athlete.

"In this poem, my intent is to present facts about Cal Norris, not to make any judgments. I am hoping the reader will have some questions about Cal. However, you will have to supply your own answers. My job isn't to attempt to explain why Cal does what he does, merely to *show* what he does. **99**

Writing Opportunity

Describe someone you know who has a unique physical talent. You might use *hyperbole* (exaggeration) to emphasize the talent.

Write about someone real or imaginary who acts in ways contrary to the expectations that others have of him or her.

REPRODUCIBLE

66 I had just finished reading something about a species that is nearing extinction. My curiosity was aroused, and I turned to the encyclopedia to find a list of extinct species.

"I decided to write a poem in which I listed several species that were nearing extinction. After playing around for a while, I decided to use rhymed quatrains.

"But poems don't always end up being about what we planned to write. 'Sitting by the Phone' ends up not being about the end of a species, but something else. And as the topic of my poem changed, the title also changed from 'Gone Forever' to 'Sitting by the Phone.' **99**

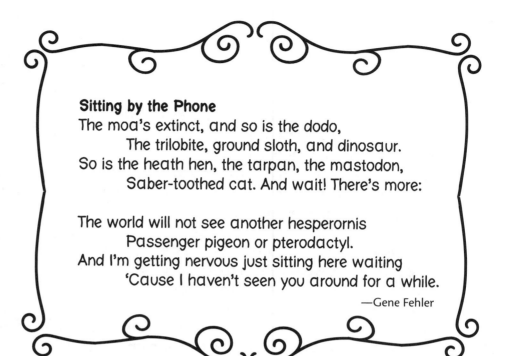

Sitting by the Phone
The moa's extinct, and so is the dodo,
    The trilobite, ground sloth, and dinosaur.
So is the heath hen, the tarpan, the mastodon,
    Saber-toothed cat. And wait! There's more:

The world will not see another hesperornis
    Passenger pigeon or pterodactyl.
And I'm getting nervous just sitting here waiting
    'Cause I haven't seen you around for a while.

—Gene Fehler

Writing Opportunity

Make several lists (e.g., types of trees, fish, desserts, hats, music, shoes, snakes, buildings). Use one of your lists as the basis for a poem. Find a way to incorporate as many of the items into your poem as possible.

Write a poem about a telephone call you received that changed your life in some way. Or write about a phone call you didn't receive that might have changed your life if you had.

© Good Apple GA13062

Modern Medicine: Pro and Con

"To cure the jaundice, eat nine lice on a
slice of bread and butter."

—from *The Book of Medical Superstitions*

The tubes and wires and shots and pills
That doctors use to treat our ills
All help provide the healing touch.
But lice, at least, don't cost as much.

—Gene Fehler

Writing Opportunity

Look through a book of quotations. Select one idea that intrigues you enough to base a poem on it. The quote might suggest a story, cause you to philosophize, or create a strong emotional response in you. Use whatever form and mood that seem appropriate to you.

A Word from the Poet

Edward Scissorhands

Snow fell from the mountain
And the girl danced in her yard.

Cold steel fingers clicked and slashed,
Sliced and cut;
His touch was never soft enough
To make him feel that he belonged.
Too many blamed him for the wrongs
He never meant nor understood.

From a castle dungeon-dark
His gift of love swirled in snowflakes
And the girl danced in her yard.

She never knew his touch again,
Yet beauty grew wherever Edward's fingers flew,
Sculpting figures white as the dress she wore
The night she kissed him, the night she left him.
No one learned how much she missed him.

Hearts are soft, and love is hard.
Snow fell from the mountain
And the girl danced in her yard.

—Gene Fehler

Writing Opportunity

Write about a character or moment from a movie you have seen. Don't worry about whether or not the reader is familiar with the movie; simply be as clear as possible in sharing what you observed.

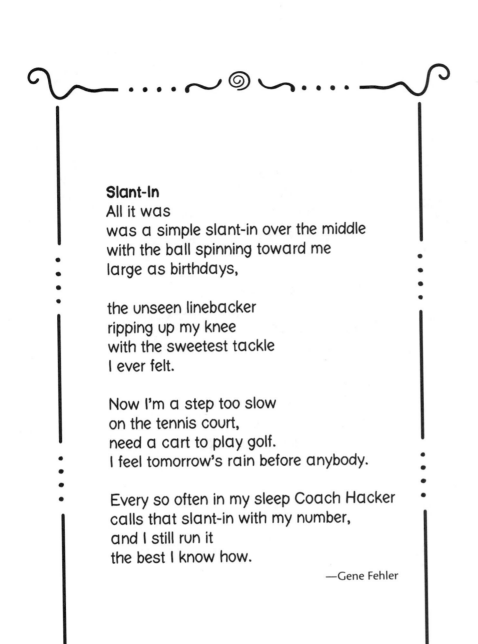

Slant-In
All it was
was a simple slant-in over the middle
with the ball spinning toward me
large as birthdays,

the unseen linebacker
ripping up my knee
with the sweetest tackle
I ever felt.

Now I'm a step too slow
on the tennis court,
need a cart to play golf.
I feel tomorrow's rain before anybody.

Every so often in my sleep Coach Hacker
calls that slant-in with my number,
and I still run it
the best I know how.

—Gene Fehler

❝ I had just finished a tennis match with a teaching colleague, Dave. We were evenly matched, although perhaps he had a slight edge in execution, and I had a slight edge in speed. I don't recall who won this particular match, but I do recall Dave explaining that he wore a knee brace because of a football injury.

"Sometime within the next few days, I recalled this line: *a step too slow on the tennis court.* Perhaps Dave had said it, or maybe I thought of it myself, but the line became the basis for this poem. As I described the experience that resulted in the loss of that crucial step, I pretended that it had happened to me. **❞**

Writing Opportunity

Write a poem about something that happened to someone else. As you write the poem, pretend it happened to you. Write it from a first-person viewpoint; try to totally immerse yourself in the situation so you can recreate the thoughts and feelings realistically.

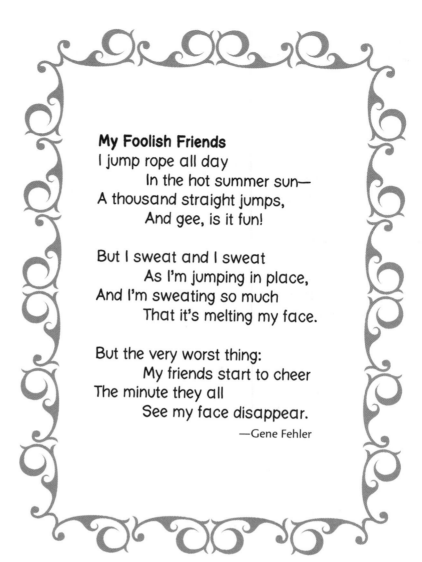

A Word from the Poet

66 While visiting a fourth-grade class, the students gave me some topics to write poems about. One topic was 'jumping rope.' As I worked on my rough draft, I tried to observe the moment—not in reality but in my imagination. I tried to observe myself jumping rope. What would I do? How would I feel?

"I tried to picture where or when I would jump rope—in the hot summer sun—and I wrote it down. If it was a hot summer day, I'd probably be sweating. And if I happened to sweat a lot, what might happen? Before you know it, observation blended with imagination and led me in directions I never expected. 99

My Foolish Friends

I jump rope all day
    In the hot summer sun—
A thousand straight jumps,
    And gee, is it fun!

But I sweat and I sweat
    As I'm jumping in place,
And I'm sweating so much
    That it's melting my face.

But the very worst thing:
    My friends start to cheer
The minute they all
    See my face disappear.

—Gene Fehler

Writing Opportunity

Describe a moment at play in a poem. What are you doing? Where or when are you doing it? Then let your imagination take over and enjoy seeing where it takes you!

Skating with Sherri

Most evenings during my tenth summer
my best friend Sherri and I roller-skated
on the sidewalk between our two houses.
Skating behind her I could watch
her long blond hair dance in the breeze
as she leaned her body left, then right,
left again, then bent forward, lunging
into a sprint toward some imaginary finish line.
We'd almost always finish side by side.

Sherri moved away with her parents
the next winter, too suddenly for me
to remember to give back the key
we always adjusted our skates with
those sweet summer nights.

I never saw her again, never even knew
where she moved to, but every so often
I see that key in a box of keepsakes.
My mind drifts back to her long blond hair,
her smile, and I think how friends
never really leave you—
not so long as there is still a key
to unlock a memory.

—Gene Fehler

❝ Some students asked me to write a poem about skating. I thought about the time when I was growing up and about my next-door neighbor, Sherri. She was my best friend, and we used to skate together. Sherri didn't really move away—I just added that to make the poem more dramatic. **❞**

Writing Opportunity

Write about a best friend and a special moment that you remember with him or her. Be sure to include the time and place where this happened.

❝ A teacher asked me to write a poem about summer. As I sat and contemplated ideas, the following line popped into my head: *Summer in its sun-drenched victory of green.* I wasn't sure which little voice hidden inside my brain thought that one up, but I liked it. 'Not a bad first line', I thought. 'Now if I only had a poem to go with it.'

"Summer . . . summer . . . I let the word sweep over me and lost myself in thoughts of summer. I drifted off into a world of half-remembered summers. After a while I realized that most of my impressions and recollections of summer centered on baseball. So it seemed only natural that my summer poem would be about baseball. I compared the baseball of my childhood summers to modern baseball summers. Modern baseball seemed different, with its domed parks and artificial turf.

"I realized that my poem would no longer be about summer itself, but the difference between how I felt about old-time and modern baseball. I changed one word in my first line and added another. It became: *Late summer in its sun-drenched dance of green.* And I went on from there. ❞

Artificial Baseball

Late summer in its sun-drenched dance of green
Stood watch outside the massive sterile dome
Where air-conditioned artificial turf
Took weary time-warped players far from home.

Past summers, in their breeze-filled victories,
Lit up the parks where players learned to read
The speed of sky, twist of cloud, slant of sun—
The language that they knew they all would need.

Now summer, in its sun-spun loneliness,
Hopes the dome will break, fears it never will.
It senses that the greatest summer game
Lies frozen in the dome's unnatural chill.

—Gene Fehler

Writing Opportunity

Now try writing your own poem about summer.

King Arthur Calling

Across a slow-spun web of centuries, Arthur speaks.
I watch his voice, sharp as Excalibur slice across
the worst part of today, ripping away time's web
until a vision grows like darkroom film: Guinevere
in her bedroom alone while outside Arthur and Lancelot
speak of trust and honor; Galahad and his dream-tossed
chase across continents for the Holy Grail, for the
Siege Perilous at the Round Table where one hundred
fifty warriors wise wait for the empty seat to fill;
to earlier images of Arthur pulling sword from stone,
and Merlin there to show the way to Camelot.
Only Arthur's breath ebbed to a standstill at Avalon,
not the voice that speaks yet of dreams, of magic,
of knights long since devoured by spiders lurking fat
in time's elaborate web.

—Gene Fehler

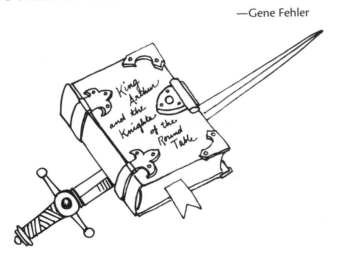

66 I was meeting with a high school class in Mobile, Alabama. I told them it was possible to write a poem about any subject; and to prove it, they should assign me a topic. I would come to class the next day with a poem about that subject. They briefly discussed possibilities as a group and decided I should write a poem about King Arthur.

"Well, my knowledge of King Arthur was essentially limited to what I'd seen in the film *Camelot* and read in scattered allusions from various pieces of literature over the years. So I took a trip to the school library and looked up *Arthur, King* in various reference books. I jotted down notes about the sword *Excalibur*, about Merlin and Lancelot and Guinevere, about Galahad and the Holy Grail, about the Round Table, and about Arthur's death at Avalon.

"That evening I sorted through my notes and tried to incorporate some of what I'd learned. When I finished my rough draft, I found that I was trying to write not merely about King Arthur, but also about a changing world where romance as found in Arthurian legends seemed gone forever. **99**

Writing Opportunity

Have someone assign you a topic. Then try to write a poem about that subject. You may have to do some research. And you may just discover the value of research in assisting and supporting your writing.

❝ A young girl asked me if I'd ever written a poem about Maine. She didn't mention the state or spell the name; she merely said the word. So, at my first opportunity, I started thinking about *main* or *Maine* and writing down whatever thoughts popped into my head, no matter how silly or off the subject they seemed to be.

"Here are my thoughts.❞

Maine Thoughts

A fourth-grade girl asks me
if I have ever written about Maine.
I think friendships: "You're my main man!"
or the ship: "Remember the *Maine!*"—
Cuba and the Spanish-American War
a hundred years ago—the Rough Riders
and Teddy Roosevelt: "Speak softly
and carry a big stick." Or even Main Street,
which in my home town was only one block long,
the place I spent my teen years,
mostly at Crandal's Cafe drinking sodas
and milk shakes with Johnny and Dale
and Lou and watching the town drunk,
Painter Bill, paint his chalk pictures on the sidewalk.
But no, she means the state, that icy cold spot
of mountains and rocky sea-lined shore
that just barely catches the northeastern-most
part of our country and hangs on for its life.
Maine, the home of Stephen King, whose tales
of horror chill us even more
than the state's long, hard winters.
Maine, where Jessica Fletcher wrote her tales
of murder to warm those TV nights.
I call it the state of Maine.
I suspect that only its most devoted natives
would be tempted to call it our country's main state.

—Gene Fehler

Writing Opportunity

Choose a state or province and start writing whatever thoughts enter your head. Don't worry about how it might end up; simply enjoy the journey that thinking about the place takes you on.

Pet-Owner

If dogs were disguised
as cats
I'd save the spoiled milk
for Sunday breakfast

and listen
for the claw-toothed
end of growls.

I'd watch them lick
the wet fur of pups
with sandpaper tongues
and eat wind-up
mice
for dessert.

If dogs were disguised
as cats
yarn would wait
forever dangling
beside sleepy summer eyes
bone-weary above cold noses
tickled by the spider web
of whiskers.

If dogs were disguised
as cats
I'd be a zookeeper
with a leash
made of tire chains
and listen to it
jingle
as the sound of
purring
put me to sleep.

—Gene Fehler

A Word from the Poet

❝ There is no story or point to this poem; it merely tries to generate some kind of picture or feeling about dogs or cats. ❞

Writing Opportunity

Write a poem about a pet you own or have owned. If you've never owned a pet, pretend you own one and write a poem about it.

A Word from the Poet

66 This didn't happen; I made it up. I tried to present a rather unpleasant moment on a baseball field. Did I succeed? **99**

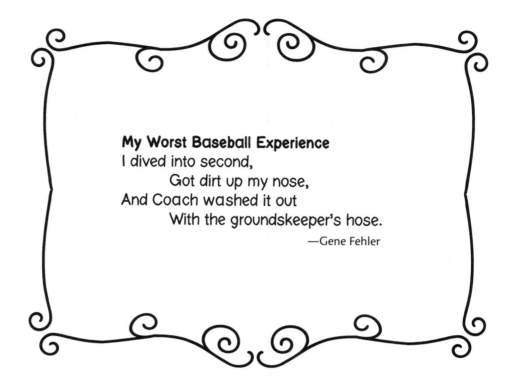

My Worst Baseball Experience
I dived into second,
    Got dirt up my nose,
And Coach washed it out
    With the groundskeeper's hose.

—Gene Fehler

Writing Opportunity

Try writing a second (and even third) verse for this poem to continue the story.

Unless you are lucky, you have probably been injured at least once in your life. Sometimes memories of injuries are still vivid. If you're up to it, recall one of those times and write about it. Show what happened and perhaps how you felt. You can make up or pretend as much as you like!

REPRODUCIBLE

Wide Receiver on the School Team
The ball was made for my hands.
Or else they were made for the ball.
I sit in class and fumble my book.
It hits the floor like a muffed punt.
A page rips when I pick it up.
Behind me, Sally Dobbs giggles.
She scribbles a note, passes it
to me. It slips from my sweating
hands. From my desktop, her words
stare up at me: "You're cute."

I take my pencil from my pocket. It
feels awkward in my long fingers. I
press its tip to the paper, trying to
make the thoughts in my head find
their way down to the pencil and out
its tip. The lead snaps. Then the
pencil falls from my fingers and I
wish I was on the football field
where my hands always do just
what my head tells them to.

—Gene Fehler

66 Sometimes we write poems about people we wished we knew—or about made-up people we would have enjoyed knowing. Sally Dobbs is one such person. She's a blend of three or four girls that I had crushes on in my school years. Though the events in these two poems never happened, they could have. I can imagine myself reacting as the football player did in 'Wide Receiver on the School Team' when Sally passed a note to him. I can imagine the joy the shortstop in 'Our Pitcher, Sally Dobbs' must have felt, walking hand in hand with Sally Dobbs. **99**

Our Pitcher, Sally Dobbs

With her cap pulled down,
shading her face and covering
her dark hair,
she looks like a boy,
but that doesn't concern her.
Or us either.

It's her pitching that matters,
the slow curves that keep
the big Carleyville sluggers off balance,
setting them up for her hard fastballs.

From shortstop I cheer her on,
then help her out of a jam
in the last inning by starting
a game-ending double play,
a play so nice she gives me
a quick hug and lets me
hold her hand
when I walk her home.

—Gene Fehler

Writing Opportunity

Invent or think of a person who you would like to know better. Describe a scene showing something that happens that brings you closer to that person.

Do you think you've said all you can say about your special person? Maybe you haven't. Notice that "Wide Receiver on the School Team" introduces us to Sally Dobbs, and "Our Pitcher, Sally Dobbs" tells us more about her. Now think of something else that you would like to tell about the special person in your first poem.

Library Tag
Summer days after baseball
we ended up down the street
at our village library.
Our sneakers did our reading.
They read the cut of grass,
slant of earth, crust of clay,
slip of sand beneath our feet
as we chased each other
outside silent walls.

Our task: to avoid
the thrown soccer ball,
to outspeed it,
deceive it,
jump over it,
to fake, feint, fool the thrower.

We slower runners found
the open doorway, a good place
to duck wild throws,
to hide against the rush
of chasing feet
when the threat of a tag
kept us always sprinting.
A day came (I never imagined it would):
I ducked in and the library caught me,
kept me there, safe from the mad rush
of screaming sneakers,
kept me chasing across
a million whispering pages
in a world where I could run
at my own speed.

—Gene Fehler

Writing Opportunity

Substitute a different season in the first line of this poem, and use it to write your own poem. You can also change other words, such as *days* to *nights* and *after* to *before* or *during*.

❝ I was a youngster during the time of the Korean War. Whenever I went to a movie theater, I would have to rush into the restroom during the newsreels and hide. War terrified me. I'd clamp my hands over my ears to try to keep out the sounds of the bombs and the shells and the guns. Death and war were my biggest childhood fears, and this poem came directly out of them. **❞**

War Beyond the Mississippi

I feared the rumbling in distant skies
beyond the waters that were the Mississippi.

A war raged across the water.
At eight years old, I knew only that.

The Mississippi, a half-mile from home,
was wide as any ocean I'd ever seen.

I rode my bike there while the sky rumbled.
I waited for a rain that never came.

Dark, dry skies told me the booming was the
same sound I heard in movie newsreels

when big planes, bombs, horrors filling the screen
sent me stumbling up the aisle to a restroom

where I clapped my hands over my ears
and pushed hard to keep the war from coming in.

At the Mississippi I watched for planes, ships,
for gray puffs from where the bombs hit.

I did not yet know it was Iowa, not Korea,
at the far edge of those mighty waters.

As the deadly shells came closer I turned,
pedaled my bike home, outracing the wind.

I could feel death closing in, war and death,
and I doubted I would ever make it to nine.

—Gene Fehler

Writing Opportunity

Write a free verse poem about a topic that is important to you or worries you. Experiment with two-line stanzas.

My Dad Taught Me
Before my dad left
he taught me how
to hold my bat
away from my body
when I swing
and how to let the ball
spin off my fingertips
when I throw
and how to oil my glove
and wrap string around it
with a ball inside
so when I sleep
the pocket will remember
the ball just as clearly
as I remember
my dad's face.

—Gene Fehler

66 Sometimes parents don't always do all the things we would like them to. I love baseball, and I first became interested in it because my dad would listen to White Sox games on the radio. But he had never played ball himself, or with me.

"After I had two sons of my own and played a lot of baseball with them, I realized how much I'd missed out on because I'd never played ball with my own dad. After he died, I wrote this fantasy poem about what I wish my dad had taught me. 99

Writing Opportunity

Make a list of things you learned from someone; then use that list in a poem. Or, write a poem about one specific thing you learned from someone. Go into detail. What did you learn? From whom? When? Where? What effect did it have on your life?

A Word from the Poet

❝ Baseball was what bound my dad and me together most closely. In his final few years, he suffered from bone cancer, but I was living with my wife and sons several hundred miles away. I didn't see him often and could not be at his bedside during his final days.

"'Deathbed Showdown' is based partly on some of the moments I spent with him then, but even more on my vision of what our final moments together should have been like. Sometimes there is no closure when a relationship ends—through death or other circumstances—and we need to create it. This poem provides necessary closure for me. **❞**

Deathbed Showdown

Death goes into its stretch,
uncoils toward the wasted body
lying on hospital sheets like a dried leaf.
The dying man sees the pitch coming,
grips his son's hand.
Then, his voice a cracked whisper,
takes his best swing:
"Remember . . . the game against Westfield,
you were twelve . . . maybe thirteen . . .
your double . . . with two out
in the last inning . . . won it.
You came through, son! You came through."
The son squeezes his father's hand,
knows the end is imminent,
knows, too, that in his father's final
moments
something has outdueled Death.

—Gene Fehler

Writing Opportunity

If you've ever visited a hospital or a waiting room in a doctor's or dentist's office, write about one or more of your recollections of that experience.

REPRODUCIBLE

Late Afternoons

when I'm alone in the house
late afternoons
before you come always angry
home from work
too tired to eat out
or even talk
before the fireplace
holding hands like we used to
I think of how it was

our sons still in school
rushing from the bus
to greet me, begging for cookies
to spoil their appetites
before our supper together
sharing games, school projects,
high school sports, that special date
plans for college
marriage

I sit sometimes
by the window now
and watch the school bus
drive right by
stopping down the street
to let off strangers
that look so familiar
late afternoons
when I'm alone in the house

—Gene Fehler

66 I wrote 'Late Afternoons' when my son Andy was in fourth grade and my son Tim was in sixth. I had such a good time with them as children that I hated to think of them someday being adults with lives of their own, perhaps thousands of miles away. I thought about the sadness that many people must feel when faced with the 'empty nest' syndrome. I thought of how doubly sad it must be for a couple who are unable to communicate.

"I wrote this from the viewpoint of a middle-aged woman whose children are now adults. They have moved away, and she has been left with only memories and an uncommunicative husband. 99

Writing Opportunity

Write about a time when you were alone or felt alone. Where were you? When was it? What caused you to feel that way?

Making Miracles

One of the things poets love most about writing is that they have the chance to make miracles happen! Writing poems gives us license to fib or exaggerate or pretend as much as we want without getting into trouble.

In a poem, we can become someone we are not or will never be in real life; we can do things we might never do and go places we can only see in our imaginations. We can meet our heroes or live our dreams, confront our fears, and save the day. We can win the race, make things better, and be the superstar.

But imagine for a moment if there were no new poets. What sadness if there were no new books of poetry to thrill us, to make us laugh, and make us cry. Imagine a world without poetry.

If Poetry Dies

The poem springs lively from the timeless page
Much like Athena, sprung from Zeus full-grown;
It arches like a gymnast, center stage,
Where grace brings beauty like we've never known.

The poem explodes with power, like a sea
Wind-blown into the sweeping height of waves.
Its every line affects our destiny:
It shocks, seduces, saddens, and it saves.

The poem, like Dorothy's cyclone, takes us all
To magic lands like Oz; it lifts us high.
It spins us, sends us soaring, makes us fall.
It shows that we, like birds, can sometimes fly.

If poems should ever lose the gift of flight
Or hang as limp as flowers in a storm,
Our world will be deprived of one vast light
That focuses our eyes and keeps us warm.

—Gene Fehler

Writing a poem gives you a chance to make a miracle.

A Final Word from the Poet

"Poets may write for different reasons, but we are all overjoyed when a reader truly likes and admires what we have written. And just think of what a great joy it would be to open a poetry book one day and see one of your poems printed there on the page! Imagine hearing your voice booming in a poem that stirs the imagination and emotions of others in a new and special way.

"Remember that we don't have to have the complete poem composed in our heads before we begin writing. If we wait for this to happen, we might go through life without ever writing one. Sometimes the key to writing a poem is getting that first line down, to begin writing even before we know what our poem will be about—or how it will end. Often you'll discover that one thought leads directly into another, and another, and soon you have a poem!

"So grab your pencil and paper or turn on your computer, and let the word play begin! Hurry before someone else writes the very poem that you want to create!

"And remember these words from the poet Dylan Thomas:

The world is never the same once a good poem has been added to it."

—*The International Thesaurus of Quotations.*
Compiled by Rhoda Thomas Tripp (Harper & Row, 1970).

Appendix

POETRY TERMS

This glossary lists some basic terms to help you write, read, and appreciate poetry.

alliteration	the repetition of the same letter at the beginning of a succession of words (e.g., *seasons of sunshine; no beech or birch*)
allusion	a reference to any person, place, or thing—fictitious, historical, or actual
antagonist	a character or force in a story or poem that is in conflict with the main character (see *protagonist*)
artistic unity	when all elements of a poem work together to achieve its central purpose
assonance	repeated vowel sounds in words (e.g., *a ground ball will bounce*)
blank verse	unrhymed poetry used in iambic pentameter
character	any person involved in a story or poem
cinquain	a specific form with 22 syllables that are divided 2–4–6–8–2 in five lines
climax	the turning point, high point, or moment of highest intensity in a plot
conflict	a clash of actions, desires, ideas, or goals in the plot of a story
consonance	repeated consonant sounds at the ends of words (e.g., *stroke of luck*)
couplet	two consecutive rhymed lines
figure of speech	way of saying one thing and meaning another (e.g., metaphor, simile)
form	the design of a poem as a whole
free verse	non-metrical verse; no definite rhythm or rhyme
haiku	a three-line poem about nature, usually 17 syllables divided 5–7–5
hyperbole	exaggeration for effect
iambic pentameter	a ten-syllable line with accents on even-numbered syllables
imagery	words or sequences of words that refer to any sensory experience
irony	a situation or use of language involving some kind of discrepancy (e.g., difference between what a character says and means, between what is expected and what really happens)
lyric	a short poem expressing thoughts and feelings of a single speaker (usually with little physical action)
metaphor	a comparison in which one thing is said to be something else (e.g., *I am the monster of the mound; the basketball is a burning coal*)
meter	the arrangement and measurement of rhythm in poetry
metrical foot	a syllabic pattern in poetry (such as the *iamb* in iambic pentameter)
narrative poem	a poem that tells a story
onomatopoeia	using words or creating phrases of words that seem to imitate sounds (e.g., *buzz, zoom, hiss, slushy, squishy, crunchy, murmur*)

 © Good Apple GA13062

POETRY TERMS

paradox	a statement that seems self-contradictory but really makes some sense
parody	imitating the style or work of another writer (usually humorous)
persona	a fictitious identity created by the author
personification	a figure of speech in which a thing, an animal, or an abstract term is given human attributes or qualities (e.g., *raindrops thud and laugh*)
plot	the sequence of events or incidents in a poem
point of view	the angle of vision or narrative viewpoint from which a poem is told
protagonist	the central character in a poem or story
quatrain	a four-line stanza
rhyme	repeated end sounds in words (e.g., *ball, hall, fall*)
rhyme scheme	any fixed pattern of rhymes characterizing a whole poem or its stanzas
rhythm	a measured pattern or cadence of sounds
setting	the time and place in which the action of a poem or story occurs
simile	a figure of speech that compares one thing to another using the words *like* or *as* (e.g., *our minds are like chalkboards*)
slant rhyme	an inexact rhyme
sonnet	fourteen-line fixed-rhyme poem in iambic pentameter
stanza	a group of lines whose metrical pattern is repeated throughout a poem; stanza groups include: *couplet*—two lines; *tercet*—three lines; *quatrain*—four lines; *quintet*—five lines; *sestet*—six lines; *septet*—seven lines; *octave*—eight lines
style	a writer's unique approach (e.g., use of language, tone, form)
suspense	the quality that makes the reader eager to discover what happens next and how a poem or story will end
symbol	something that means *more* than what it is; an object, person, situation, or action that suggests other meanings
theme	the central idea or unifying generalization implied or stated by a poem or story
tone	the attitude expressed toward a subject
understatement	implying more than what is said
verse	metrical writing; sometimes synonymous with *poetry*

POEMS IN
Let the Poems Begin!

PUBLICATION CREDITS

Poems in *Let the Poems Begin!* originally appeared in the following publications:

The Advocate; Alalitcom; Aldebaran; Alive Now!; Austin Poetry Sampler; Bellowing Ark; A Book of the Year; Booklist; Bristlecone; Capper's Weekly; Celebration; Circus Maximus; The Color Green; Eclectic Man; Elysian Fields Quarterly; English Journal; Faith 'n Stuff; Fan Magazine; Footwork; Green Feather; Green's Magazine; Harp-Strings; Home Education Magazine; Home Times; Horizons; If We'd Wanted Quiet We'd Have Raised Goldfish: Poems for Parents (Meadowbrook Press); The Illinois Architectural and Historical Review; In My Shoes; The Inkling; Instructor Magazine; Janus-Scth; Light; Light Year '86 (Bits Press); Lighten Up! (Meadowbrook Press); The Lyric; Magical Blend; Minneapolis Review of Baseball; Mixed Bag; Mother's Today; Mt. Vernon Herald; Murderous Intent; Nerve Bundle Review; The New Press Literary Review; Nexus; Oasis; Olden Times; Once Upon a World; Opossum Holler Tarot; Pacific Coast Journal; The Panhandler; Parnassus Literary Journal; Pennywhistle Press; Phase and Cycle; Poems: Prairie Style; Poet Lore; The Poetry Peddler; Poet's Pen Quarterly; Point; Potpourri; Quad-City Times; The Quill; Red Owl; Rockford Morning Star; The Rose's Hope; The Roswell Literary Review; Second Glance; Semi-Dwarf Review; Song, Shoofly, Sleuth Journal; Southern Style; Spitball; Sports Illustrated for Kids; SPSM&H; Sun Dog; Sunrust; Thirteen; Timelapse; Voices International; Whitewater Woman; Wind; Without Halos; Write On; Writer's Gazette; Writer's Journal; Zone 3.

Also, poems were originally published in the following books:
Center Field Grasses: Poems from Baseball, McFarland & Company, Inc.: Jefferson, NC, 1991.
I Hit the Ball! Baseball Poems for the Young, McFarland & Company, Inc.: Jefferson, NC, 1996.